SCHOOL IMPROVEMENT
for the NEXT GENERATION

STEPHEN WHITE
RAYMOND L. SMITH

Solution Tree | Press

a division of

Solution Tree

555 North Morton Street
Bloomington, IN 47404
800.733.6786 (toll free) / 812.336.7700
FAX: 812.336.7790

email: info@solution-tree.com
solution-tree.com

Printed in the United States of America

14 13 12 11 10   1 2 3 4 5

FSC
Mixed Sources
Product group from well-managed
forests and other controlled sources
Cert no. SW-COC-002283
www.fsc.org
© 1996 Forest Stewardship Council

Library of Congress Cataloging-in-Publication Data

White, Stephen H., 1949-
    School improvement for the next generation / Stephen White, Raymond L. Smith.
        p. cm.
    Includes bibliographical references and index.
    ISBN 978-1-935249-20-7 (perfect bound) -- ISBN 978-1-935249-31-3 (library bound) 1. School improvement programs--United States. I. Smith, Raymond L. II. Title.
    LB2822.82.W555 2010
    371.2'07--dc22
                                    2009052845

Solution Tree
Jeffrey C. Jones, CEO & President

Solution Tree Press
President: Douglas M. Rife
Publisher: Robert D. Clouse
Vice President of Production: Gretchen Knapp
Managing Production Editor: Caroline Wise
Copy Editor: Rachel Rosolina
Proofreader: Sarah Payne-Mills
Text Designer: Raven Bongiani
Cover Designer: Amy Shock

To my daughter, Elizabeth, whose love of life and learning is an inspiration. To our grandchildren, Yohannon, Kaitlin, Allan, Carter, Lilyana, Courtney, and Breah—you are each our joy! Finally, to the love of my life, Linda, for her patient understanding of what it takes to see ideas take flight.

—Stephen White

For Marek and Silas, who constantly inspire me to work at work worth doing. Many thanks to Julie, my best friend, my wife, and my companion, for her love, support, and encouragement throughout the writing process. Her insightful contributions to this very important work were invaluable as they helped to complete my thoughts, fill in the gaps to my thinking when my own thoughts failed me, and provide a touchstone against which school improvement concepts were tested. I also wish to thank my coauthor for the many hours of reflection, the rich dialogue, his wise council in the writing process, and for his support to engage in work worth doing. Rarely do we find individuals who willingly engage in hard, solid thinking about thinking, which was foundational to this project and to our work together.

—Raymond L. Smith

Acknowledgments

Many in the field have informed our work and graciously contributed their ideas and experiences to this volume. Steve Achronovich, Karen Cencula, Jean Creasbaum, Kristie Stutsman, Lisa Lantrip, Lonnie Garris, John Hill, Arlene Lewis, Nicole Law, Ruth Mattingley, Dawn Montgomery, Janice Montgomery, Karen Olker, Judy Stegemann, Tom Springborn, Wayne Stubbs, John Taylor, and Sue Zook have shared their stories and their insights, and we are indebted to them not only for assisting us, but more for all they do to make a difference in the lives of young people.

We also want to acknowledge Douglas Reeves, whose insights helped us understand the potential of planning, implementation, and monitoring that began on a napkin at a coffee shop on a cold winter's day in Colorado in 2004, and resulted in a deeper and more precise understanding of how leadership in school improvement can actually predict improved achievement.

Solution Tree Press would like to thank the following reviewers:

Paul Doyle
Superintendent of Schools
Paris Special School District
Fairview, Tennessee

William B. Hall
Director of Educational Leadership and Professional Development
Brevard Public Schools
Viera, Florida

Sara Ray Stoelinga
Senior Research Analyst
Consortium on Chicago School Research, University of Chicago
Chicago, Illinois

Table of Contents

About the Authors

DR. STEPHEN WHITE is executive director of Research, Accountability, and Program Evaluation for Denver Public Schools, a leading urban district committed to closing achievement gaps and reframing the paradigm of teaching and learning. His deep experience as a public school administrator—twenty years—includes service as a superintendent, assistant superintendent, executive director, CEO of a higher education Board of Cooperative Educational Services, high school principal, and coordinator of special education.

Dr. White also served as senior professional development associate with the Leadership and Learning Center™ from 2003 to 2010, and has provided expertise in data analysis, systems, leadership assessment, program evaluation, and school improvement to help change the way educators view themselves and manage data in an era of high-stakes accountability and testing.

In addition to *School Improvement for the Next Generation*, Dr. White has authored *Leadership Maps* (2009), *Beyond the Numbers* (2005), *Show Me the Proof* (2005), twenty articles, and two invited chapters for bestselling authors, including the book *Ahead of the Curve* (2007). Dr. White brings over thirty-five years of experience at all levels, is the primary author of the PIM™ school improvement framework and the Leadership Map, and has reviewed over 2,300 school improvement plans since 2005. He is active in his church, The Rock, Real Community, in Castle Rock, Colorado, and lives with his lovely wife, Linda. Together, they have eight children and seven grandchildren.

DR. RAYMOND L. SMITH was a public school educator for thirty-four years, serving as a teacher, principal, and director of secondary education, and has taught graduate course work. He is a professional development associate with the Leadership and Learning Center in Englewood, Colorado. He travels throughout the United States to assist school systems in implementing best practices related to leadership development, change, executive coaching, and school improvement planning. Dr. Smith has done extensive research and implementation on school improvement practices. Toward that end, he served as a co-primary researcher on a team who conducted the original Planning, Implementation and Monitoring (PIM) Study for the Leadership and Learning Center. The PIM Study was highlighted in Douglas Reeves' book, *The Learning Leader: How to Focus School Improvement for Better Results* (2006).

Dr. Smith has authored several learning modules for the Ohio Leadership Advisory Council, which are intended for use by superintendents, district leadership team members, and building leadership team members, as well as by others such as central office personnel, principals, teachers, related services personnel, and school board members interested in improving instructional practice and achievement for all students. The modules are aligned with essential practices outlined in Ohio's *Leadership Development Framework* (Ohio Leadership Advisory Council, 2008). Dr. Smith primary motivation is to be a force for positive change and to inspire others to greatness. He holds an MA in educational administration and earned his PhD in educational leadership and innovation from the University of Colorado Health Sciences Center in Denver, Colorado. He lives with his wife Julie in Pacific City, Oregon.

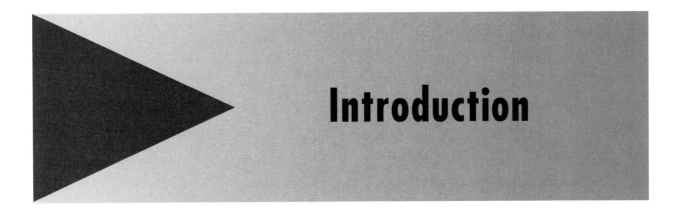

Introduction

How wonderful it is that nobody need wait a
single moment before starting to improve the
world.

—Anne Frank

School improvement in its current form is ubiquitous in public and private schools in Canada, the United States, Australia, New Zealand, the United Kingdom, and Singapore, as well as most developed nations around the world. For North Americans, at least a generation has passed since the wholesale adoption of school improvement planning as a means to improve student achievement and build capacity among staff. A number of school improvement models identify the attributes that increase student achievement, the most notable being Larry Lezotte's seven Correlates of Effective Schools, which were updated in 2008 to reflect refinements in the process. The correlates continue to offer a solid and consistent framework for school improvement. Other models such as Schools that Learn (Senge, 2000), Success for All (Eide, 2001), and Coalition of Essential Schools (Sizer, 2004) have influenced school improvement practices and state and district improvement templates for decades. A 2004 innovation is the PIM school improvement process (Reeves, et al. 2007), which identifies planning, implementation, and monitoring as distinct phases of school improvement and school change (see appendix A for sample rubrics from the PIM framework). Each phase is supported by deep research in leading change, educational reform, high-yield instructional strategies, data analysis, collaboration, and strategic planning (Boyatzis & McKee, 2005; Casciaro & Lobo, 2005; DuFour, Eaker, & DuFour, 2005; Elmore, 2004; Fernandez, 2006; Fullan, Hill, & Crévola, 2006; Marzano, Waters, & McNulty, 2005; Pfeffer & Sutton, 2000, 2006; Reeves, 2004a, 2004b, 2006, 2008b; Reeves et al., 2007; Rushkoff, 2005; Schmoker, 2006; Surowiecki, 2004; Wenglinsky, 2002; White, 2005a).

For this book, we applied our experience reviewing thousands of written plans, as well as supporting schools and district officials in carrying out these plans, to identify the critical best practices, approaches, and antecedent conditions necessary for the next generation of school improvement efforts. Schools will need the added clarity in focus and delivery that this volume provides in order to meet the changing needs of students; respond to new dynamics in technology, teaching, and how schools are structured and operated; and maintain a cohesive focus that is predictive of improved achievement and narrowing of student gaps. Collaboration is critical, but not enough in itself, and must be used smartly to improve the quality and efficiency of planning, implementation, monitoring, and evaluation. Accountability is also critical, but unlikely to yield the necessary gains or to inform school practitioners unless it is embedded in a comprehensive framework and practical cycle of improvement, as this book outlines.

School Improvement for the Next Generation changes the school improvement emphasis from creating an improvement cycle to refining the quality of that cycle, with clearly defined planning, implementation, monitoring, and evaluation protocols undergirded by extensive collaboration and accountability. We draw on these next-generation components to examine school improvement in a new light for a new era.

A conservative estimate of the number of professional hours spent developing and publishing school improvement plans since the early 1980s is staggering, representing several thousand dollars each year for the smallest of schools. With over one hundred thousand schools in the United States alone, one has to ask, has the investment been worth the effort? What changes have occurred in terms of student achievement? To what degree has this collaborative process raised the level of professionalism? Has the profession been informed by the lessons learned through school improvement? In 2004, we embarked on a journey to answer these questions through an extensive review of school improvement plans across the continent. The first generation of school improvement plans established a foundation for change that offers today's educators an opportunity that prior generations did not enjoy: widespread, collaborative, shared decision making with broad stakeholder representation in which parents and students are accepted team members. The first generation introduced the need for measurable goals, exclusive accountability, and aligned district and school efforts—often for the first time. The process reminded schools everywhere to step back and establish their vision: what they wanted to achieve, why, and when. Finally, first-generation school improvement offered educators a means to introduce innovations and determine their effectiveness. These huge changes set the stage for a second generation, or second order, of improvement. We are all indebted to those pioneers who have brought us thus far.

School Improvement for the Next Generation is designed to address a few fundamental shifts in thinking and practice that will allow schools to achieve ambitious goals that have been elusive in the past. In subsequent chapters, we examine practical and proven ways schools and school districts can close achievement gaps while serving all students with greater clarity and deeper implementation.

Chapter 1 introduces a hypothetical high school—Kelly County High School—that experiences very real challenges in school improvement. In addition, it reviews the school improvement literature to provide the reader with ample evidence to warrant a sea change in school improvement efforts—one that requires the shifts in thinking described in the Kelly County High School scenario to meet the needs of all students in this increasingly complex new century. Readers will also become acquainted with colleagues who are learning to utilize this familiar mechanism to raise the bar in terms of both achievement and teaching.

Chapter 2 describes the inherent challenges of school improvement and the difficulty educators face in managing competing priorities and limiting the scope of the improvement plan to a few critical targets that will change practice. Implicit in school improvement for the next generation is the ability of the school improvement process to not only accomplish goals in terms of student achievement but to build capacity and shape a culture as well.

Chapter 3 describes the planning process and the importance of gathering data from multiple sources ensuring a solid process of inquiry that yields powerful SMART goals targeted to meet the needs of specific students. School improvement efforts are only as focused and effective as the data used to inform the design of the plan and the goals that describe a preferred outcome at the end of the improvement cycle.

Chapter 4 describes the necessary ingredients and strategies for deep implementation that are designed not only to introduce and establish best practices but sustain them. Master plan design, targeted instructional strategies, and focused and supported professional development are described holistically rather than as separate elements of school improvement, enabling schools to respond with agility to the changing needs of students and changing requirements and challenges for teachers. Examples from champion school systems illustrate the power of pursuing best practices in school improvement as relentlessly as educators have pursued the most effective classroom practices and strategies.

Chapter 5 delineates the importance and purpose of monitoring, its common pitfalls, and the reasons monitoring is as important to school improvement as feedback is to classroom learning. Sample strategies from districts in the United States and Canada illustrate what will be needed in order to succeed during the next generation of school improvement.

Chapter 6 describes the evaluation process in school improvement as a process that systematically identifies lessons learned and subsequent next steps needed to apply that learning. We suggest that this component of school improvement has been the least utilized to improve achievement and establish best practices. The evaluation cycle is examined from a practical perspective to help practitioners learn as much from school improvement processes as can be learned from solid item analysis of student achievement.

Chapter 7 describes how school improvement is itself an opportunity for leaders to establish credibility, refine innovations, develop expertise, and mentor and coach others in leadership development. This chapter describes the unique attributes of school improvement that make it the key unit of educational reform in terms of leadership development, collaborative inquiry, and application of action research at the classroom level.

Chapter 8 makes a frontal assault on initiative overload and ambitious but unattainable school improvement plans that attempt to do too much too quickly with too little. This chapter offers readers a compelling rationale to do more by attempting less, and offers explicit strategies to not only achieve excellence but continue to raise the bar in terms of rigor, cross-curricular integration, and deep schoolwide implementation.

Chapter 9 frames the emerging best practices in school improvement as an opportunity for discovery and substantive action research in every school and school district. We encourage readers to capitalize on the level of expertise that exists within their schools and districts to improve professional practice and sustain gains in student achievement. Throughout this volume, readers will recognize themselves in the skill and talents of our hypothetical high school principal and faculty, as well as extensive examples from practitioners in the field who have discovered the potential in a new look, a fresh look, a next-generation look at the process known as school improvement.

We believe your own sense of urgency will be heightened as a result of this book, and that you will join with us in calling for a renewed effort to improve schools that takes no more time and certainly no more effort than is expended today.

1 ▶ The Promise and Potential

G o on, lean in. Listen, you hear it?—Carpe— hear it?—Carpe, carpe diem, seize the day boys, make your lives extraordinary.

—Robin Williams as John Keating in **Dead Poets Society**

AUGUST 15, 2:15 P.M. Kelly County High School was a pretty amazing place to work, and Byron Johnson knew he'd found the perfect job when he was appointed principal twenty-one years ago. As he maneuvered the halls three days into the new school year, he reflected on how he had never looked back since that first day. Every year, he had the privilege of convening an amazing and select group of faculty and community members to serve on his school improvement leadership team, and every year he came away impressed by their ideas and professional accomplishments. Suddenly he heard a voice.

"Mr. Johnson, Mr. Johnson, please wait up."

She was a familiar-looking student, but he couldn't recall her name.

"My dad told me to be sure to introduce myself and say how thrilled he was that you were still our principal."

Byron tried to make the connection, but before he could ask the diminutive freshman with freckles and red hair about her father, she rescued him.

"You remember my dad, Yohannon Olsen, don't you? I'm Shaka."

"Of course," Byron replied, making the connection. "Yohannon would stop by my office every day after seventh period to ask if there was anything I needed. He helped me by making copies, running messages, even making calls for me. From his junior year when your dad moved to town until he graduated, I had my own private assistant. He attended the University of Chicago and pursued physics, right? I had no idea that you and your family even lived anywhere close to Kelly County."

"Yes, sir, we just moved back from Palo Alto because my dad took a job with the state for something to do with physics. He said he wanted me and my younger brothers to have the chance to attend Kelly."

"Wow, Shaka, you have made my day. Would you ask your dad to call me? And I would be honored if you would drop by my office periodically just to visit about your classes and interests. Would you do that for me?"

Shaka blushed a little, but Byron could tell the invitation meant something.

"Bye, Mr. Johnson."

It was Dr. Johnson now, but that didn't matter. Byron smiled at other anxious freshmen as he proceeded to the conference room.

For most of his tenure, school improvement had been incredibly fun; Byron used the process to promote the creative ideas of teachers representing a diverse faculty of 117 licensed staff. One year, the process helped the marching band successfully compete to perform at the Rose Bowl. His science teachers had an ongoing relationship with the National Aeronautics and Space Administration (NASA) that resulted in several field trips to Florida and California to witness shuttle launches and returns, as well as direct communication with several teams of astronauts in real time while they orbited hundreds of miles above Kelly County High School. The district, and indeed the entire state, was well funded, and as he reflected on his tenure this particular August afternoon, Byron had a sense of contentment that his school never lacked for resources or ideas. He entered the large conference room, complete with state-of-the-art electronics that could compete with Fortune 500 companies. Carol, as usual, had created notebooks for the yearlong commitment teachers made to serve on this committee, and they lay neatly at all eighteen chairs around the large oval conference table, along with pens engraved with "Kelly County High School: Home of the Spartans." A few members were already assembling; Byron liked to be at least fifteen minutes early to make sure everything was ready, as well as to be available and accessible to team members.

This August kickoff was different, however. Although Kelly County continued to receive accolades for student and staff performance, the school failed to make adequate yearly progress

(AYP) in sixteen of thirty-two subgroups (see bolded cells in table 1.1), even though schoolwide performance continued to be very high overall.

Table 1.1: Kelly County High School State Graduation Examination

Student Group	No. of Students	Percent of Student Body	Mathematics Proficiency		Reading/Language Arts Proficiency	
			Last Year	This Year	Last Year	This Year
African American Males	16	1.0	59%	**55%**	61%	**57%**
African American Females	19	1.2	71%	78%	75%	78%
Asian Males	42	2.6	96%	99%	94%	98%
Asian Females	59	3.7	92%	100%	95%	99%
Caucasian Males	645	40.5	83%	85%	87%	88%
Caucasian Females	687	43.2	87%	89%	89%	91%
English as a Second Language (ESL) Males	51	3.2	83%	88%	61%	**70%**
English as a Second Language (ESL) Females	61	3.8	79%	88%	72%	**71%**
Hispanic Males	47	2.9	61%	**61%**	54%	**55%**
Hispanic Females	62	3.9	76%	80%	70%	78%
Native American Males	15	0.3	44%	**39%**	49%	**47%**
Native American Females	19	0.6	73%	87%	66%	77%
Free and Reduced Lunch (FRL) Males	81	5.1	60%	**60%**	68%	**64%**
Free and Reduced Lunch (FRL) Females	61	3.8	61%	**66%**	72%	**69%**
Special Education (IEP) Males	51	3.2	30%	**34%**	44%	**43%**
Special Education (IEP) Females	32	2.0	48%	**45%**	55%	**47%**
Totals (some multiple groups)	1591		79.6%	82.5%	82%	83.5%

These issues served to tarnish an otherwise stellar reputation as a high school that could compete with the best and brightest. To comply with No Child Left Behind (NCLB), the minimum percentage of students needed to meet or exceed AYP for all student subgroups for the coming year increased 3.6 percent (from 68.5 percent to 72.1 percent) for reading/language arts and 3.8 percent (from 70.3 percent to 74.1 percent) for mathematics. As always, student subgroup gaps were expected to narrow considerably or at least show a 10 percent growth in the number of students meeting proficiency in order to avoid sanctions under NCLB.

"Most of you have seen this data already in the *Gazette*, and there is plenty to celebrate about our graduation exam results," Byron opened. "However, there is also plenty of opportunity for improvement, and we owe it to our kids, our community, and ourselves to make whatever changes are necessary going forward."

Mary, who was president of the parent teacher association at Kelly County, interrupted, "Byron, I am so sick of the way the paper emphasizes our struggles while we continue to be one of the highest-performing schools in the state, if not the country."

Byron smiled. "Thanks, Mary, and you are right. The problem is that as successful as we have been, many of our students are not showing gains."

Bill, the teacher association president, jumped in. "We continue to be judged as if all kids learn the same. Does anyone really believe that I should subject IEP students to Shakespeare in my English literature classes? The notion that all of those kids will be proficient is ludicrous."

Now it was Helen's turn: "We have had this conversation virtually every year I have been here." The entire team chuckled, as Helen was completing her thirty-sixth and final year at Kelly. "We know our externals don't always make sense, but I have no illusions about changing society or the state department or the federal government or our own legislature in the next nine months. The fact is, we can do better, and selfishly, I want to go out knowing we are as good as we think we are. I want to know we can turn the corner for that small group of students for whom Kelly isn't currently a great place to go to school."

Byron was thrilled with the level of discourse and candor around the table as Helen's comments sunk in. Some teachers looked down at their notebooks while others pensively looked at Helen; the brief silence was deafening.

Bill broke the ice by saying, "Helen, why do you have to make such good sense all the time?" The whole room erupted in laughter, a perfect segue for Byron.

"As you know, I've asked several of you to draft sections of this year's plan to give us a head start on the work we have to accomplish this year. We are going to use achievement results for identified subgroups as our measure of success, and we are going to make sure we listen to our data to get beyond the numbers and craft the smartest, most powerful strategies we can. As is our practice, these drafts are incomplete until we, as a team, modify them, replace them, start over, or do whatever we need to so that when we present the plan to our faculty, we own it and believe in it. I want to thank Jose, Kim, Mi Lai, and Bill for their willingness to gather the data, analyze it, and draft goals and strategies to get the job done again this year. Is there anything I need to clarify before you break into your assigned teams?" Silence replied. "All right, we will reconvene around 5:15, and review over dinner. Thanks so much for participating in this critical work."

Byron was pleased that the process was messy, and that the team was comfortable revising elements and challenging one another's ideas. He had learned the value of collaboration as, year after year, some departments always found a reason to resist implementing anything schoolwide. When initiatives were developed by this collaborative team, people were much more apt to implement them than mandates from the administration. The culture recognized one's participation on this committee as an honor, and two school board members used membership as a springboard to run for office. That afternoon, Byron drove to get coffee with Shaka's father, his former student Yohannon Olsen. He was proud of the progress his school had made as a professional learning community (PLC).

The next month was the best opening of school Byron had experienced since coming to the district. Very few schedule changes were necessary; there were no major changes or crises at the central office, and the football team was undefeated after three games. Byron was certain that this year would be different—this year, achievement gaps would close, and the school would become the learning organization he had worked for two decades to create. Unfortunately, this accomplished principal and his devoted leadership team would find their efforts compromised by competing priorities, lack of clarity, unexpected events, sloppy data collection and monitoring, weak implementation, and weaker evaluation of the entire process. Their adherence to conventional wisdom about school improvement would be insufficient to significantly change classroom practice and achieve their goals, despite the recognition of significant learning gaps.

SEPTEMBER 12, 12:30 P.M. "Byron, Shaka is so enjoying KCHS," Dr. Olsen said, handing the waiter back the menu, "but tell me how the school has changed since I graduated." The bushy-haired physicist had been speaking about work with molecular fusion and how the Department of Homeland Security turned to him to develop forensic maps to trace viral "fingerprints" during an epidemic. Dr. Olsen formed a consulting company that allowed him to work from anywhere, with rare face-to-face meetings in Washington, San Francisco, New York, and Beijing. "I know people and faces are different, but I want to know how education has improved."

"Well, technology has really helped us," Byron replied. "You would appreciate how knowledge has increased. Did you know we work closely with NASA each year, and our students have interned in Cape Canaveral and Houston?"

"Right, I was aware of that. Please go on." They both smiled, and Byron remembered the shorter, freckle-faced, awkward young man of a generation ago.

"We have become much more collaborative, and our decisions are informed more by data than ever before. We examine student assessments for patterns and trends and use data to drive schedules, elective offerings, and our school improvement plan." Byron paused, wondering where his former student's question was leading.

Dr. Olsen nodded. "The reason I'm asking is that I began my career by relying on detailed, rational, and strategic improvement plans that projected gains over time, but as technology and the knowledge explosion converged, my clients came to expect me to identify solutions that predict improvement short term. It is as if my work as a physicist and my grasp of engineering and molecular structure are now secondary to my professional judgment about cause-and-effect variables external to pure science. I just wondered how this explosive change in knowledge and technology has affected the world of teaching and learning."

The waiter brought the salads, and as proud as Byron was of his school's accomplishments, even of the graduate in front of him, he felt a lot like Rip Van Winkle, wondering what he'd missed all these years.

Later, driving back to campus, Byron began to self-assess the degree to which his work had been influenced by the changes around him, and whether the improvement plans his teams had developed over the years had actually changed much at all.

Dr. Byron Johnson was a skilled education leader with the heart and desire to get it right for all his students. He built an exceptionally loyal and accomplished faculty who pursued excellence at every turn, and his team was savvy to the need to respectfully engage educators in the formulation and execution of improvement plans. The promise of school improvement that began at KCHS with great enthusiasm and insight about student learning and powerful teaching would need a new set of skills, protocols, and structures to realize its potential.

A Backward Glance: Change Versus Improvement

School improvement has provided schools like KCHS with a valuable and practical tool to examine and respond to the local needs of students and staff. Most school improvement templates mirror an action research cycle: first invite consensus and active participation from students, staff, and stakeholders, and then empower participants to develop strategies or select programs of their choosing. As a result, *change* is much easier to effect than real *improvement*. Like our physicist, educators have also had to respond to unanticipated changes, and, like our principal, many have had to find ways to augment the traditional school improvement process to meet the needs of a changing population. The school improvement process, as introduced a generation ago, offers considerable benefit and potential to every school and every district that utilizes it, and this chapter examines how school improvement developed and the degree to which it has been successful—and unsuccessful—not only in terms of introducing and experimenting with change, but also in terms of improving instruction, leadership, and learning.

The National Assessment of Educational Progress (NAEP) and Trends in International Mathematics and Science Study (TIMSS) track student achievement across rural, urban, and suburban environments, and despite some encouraging shifts in terms of closing the achievement gap after the turn of the twenty-first century, the cumulative efforts of school improvement have produced minimal gains even after almost four decades (Gonzalez et al., 2004; Grigg, Lauko, & Brockway, 2006).

Schmoker (2006, pp. 34–35) refers to "the mirage of school improvement planning," while Mintrop, MacLellan, and Quintero (2001) find that school improvement plans serve largely symbolic purposes, either as rallying points for communication or as public posturing. To understand the shifts needed for the next generation of school improvement planning, we begin by reviewing historical research on school improvement.

Historical Efforts to Improve Schools

Since the 1970s, there has been a steady effort to improve U.S. schools and raise student achievement. Similar efforts are evident in numerous other countries throughout the world (Ylimaki, Jacobson, & Drysdale, 2007). The irony is, after more than thirty years of education research and a myriad of improvement efforts, a clear consensus on how to get the job done has yet to emerge. Faced with the challenge of ensuring that all students achieve high standards for learning, schools need clear leadership and support on how best to develop, engage in, and sustain lasting, effective improvement efforts. Sashkin and Egermeier (1993) provide a constructive lens into the history of school improvement efforts by analyzing policy approaches to school change and identifying four eras that are depicted in figure 1.1.

Fix the Parts	1970s
Fix the People	1980s
Fix the School	1990s
Fix the System	2000s

Figure 1.1: Changing school improvement policy approaches.
Sashkin & Egermeier, 1993

The "fix the parts" era promoted the adoption of proven innovations to address practices that were not perceived to be working. This included teaching strategies and work schedules, as well as resource capacity such as the number of library books and recommended staffing ratios.

The "fix the people" era suggested that improvement required influencing individuals to change their practices, behaviors, attitudes, and values or beliefs. This approach focused on the training and development of people, typically through legislation and external leverage from the state, province, school board, or school district to force individuals to adopt the change, including licensure requirements and preservice university course requirements.

The "fix the school" era focused on improving the problem-solving capabilities of school organizations. That is, the school, rather than the programs or people, was seen as the unit to change; educators attempted to develop the capacity of the school to solve their own problems. School improvement teams would then lead the school improvement efforts, it was believed, by applying their new knowledge and skills. This stage was widespread by the 1990s.

The latest era, "fix the system," targeted improvement efforts through comprehensive restructuring to integrate all three approaches as a "real promise for successful change in schools"

(Sashkin & Egermeier, 1993, p. 14). This approach to school improvement was a natural outgrowth of systems-thinking models that recognized the interdependent nature of events in which a single change in one part impacts all other parts (Anderson, 1993; Banathy, 1996; Jenlink, 1995; Senge, 1990). By the turn of the last century, "fix the system" was well established as the appropriate policy route to improve schools.

The four approaches to school improvement range in order of magnitude from targeting selected parts of the system in isolation to whole-school efforts of reform. Districts, states, provinces, ministries of education, and schools embraced the "fix the system" approach to make fundamental changes in how schools operate. Congress appropriated $150 million in 1998 to promote research-based schoolwide reform programs—such as Direct Instruction, High Schools That Work, and Success for All—through the Comprehensive School Reform Demonstration Program. Each model sought to put an end to fragmented, quick-fix solutions. However, Kidron and Darwin (2007) have determined that only a handful of these well-intended programs had a positive impact on overall academic achievement, as depicted in table 1.2.

Table 1.2: Rating Whole-School Improvement Models

Level	Model	Rating
Elementary	Direct Instruction (full immersion)	Moderately strong evidence
	Success for All	Moderately strong evidence
	Accelerated Schools PLUS	Moderate evidence
	America's Choice School Design	Moderate evidence
	Core Knowledge	Moderate evidence
	Literacy Collaborative	Moderate evidence
	National Writing Project	Moderate evidence
	School Development Program	Moderate evidence
	School Renaissance	Moderate evidence
Secondary	America's Choice School Design	Moderate evidence
	First Things First	Moderate evidence
	School Development Program	Moderate evidence
	Success for All—Middle School	Moderate evidence
	Talent Development High Schools	Moderate evidence

Kidron & Darwin, 2007

While only a few programs produced evidence of academic achievement recognized as moderate or moderately strong, many other whole-school reform models discussed in reform literature demonstrated only limited evidence of impact:

- ATLAS Communities
- Pearson Achievement Solutions
- Ventures Initiative
- Modern Red Schoolhouse
- Focus System
- Expeditionary Learning
- KIPP
- Middle Start
- More Effective Learning
- Different Ways of Knowing
- Integrated Thematic Instruction
- Coalition of Effective Schools
- High Schools That Work
- Making Middle Grades Work
- Onward to Excellence II
- Turning Points
- First Steps (Kidron & Darwin, 2007)

Worse yet, other whole-school models demonstrated zero evidence of impact on student achievement:

- Breakthrough to Literacy
- Coalition of Essential Schools
- Community for Learning
- Comprehensive Early Literacy Learning (Kidron & Darwin, 2007)

The development of a school improvement plan is widely seen as an "integral part of every successful ongoing individual school improvement effort" (Doud, 1995, p. 175). By 2000, most U.S. schools had school improvement plans on file at their respective state departments of education (see table 1.3, page 14).

School Improvement Defined

School improvement is often used to describe virtually every aspect of school reform. For the purposes of this volume, we use the following definition: "School improvement is a distinct approach to educational change that aims to enhance student outcomes as well as strengthen the school's capacity for managing change" (Hopkins, 2001, p. 13).

Hopkins (2001) views school improvement as the process of "focusing on the teaching-learning process and the conditions that support it" (p. 13). School improvement should be distinct, meaning that each phase should focus on specific improvements and actual change in educational practice. It should aim not only to improve student achievement, but also to build capacity and sustainability in the skill and knowledge of educational professionals. School improvement, then, is both a structure and a process. As we examine the literature on school improvement and the responses of states, provinces, and national ministries, readers are encouraged to determine the degree to which research emphasizes improved student achievement or improved capacity building, or both.

Table 1.3: Percentage of Public Schools With a Formal Improvement Plan

Location	Percentage of Schools	Location	Percentage of Schools
All 50 States and DC	88.2	Missouri	94.2
Alabama	94.3	Montana	60.2
Alaska	68.5	Nebraska	93.8
Arizona	78.3	Nevada	90.0
Arkansas	93.7	New Hampshire	71.0
California	89.5	New Jersey	76.8
Colorado	91.4	New Mexico	94.6
Connecticut	78.4	New York	70.4
Delaware	91.0	North Carolina	99.0
District of Columbia	94.3	North Dakota	99.1
Florida	97.9	Ohio	86.8
Georgia	99.6	Oklahoma	91.3
Hawaii	97.9	Oregon	100
Idaho	79.3	Pennsylvania	56.9
Illinois	96.8	Rhode Island	100
Indiana	96.1	South Carolina	92.2
Iowa	92.3	South Dakota	53.3
Kansas	99.8	Tennessee	99.7
Kentucky	96.5	Texas	97.3
Louisiana	98.3	Utah	81.4
Maine	63.7	Vermont	97.5
Maryland	98.6	Virginia	88.2
Massachusetts	96.1	Washington	93.7
Michigan	96.8	West Virginia	96.5
Minnesota	68.3	Wisconsin	57.7
Mississippi	85.7	Wyoming	100

National Center for Education Statistics, 2000

Research on Planning Effectiveness

Planning calls for a "learning agenda" (Boyatzis & McKee, 2005, p. 101) to set priorities, establish goals, identify strategies, and obtain commitment from staff and other stakeholders (Bernhardt, 1999). Phillips and Moutinho (2000) conclude that there is but a small amount of empirical research on the measurement of strategic planning effectiveness. For example, in a study of 127 Kentucky school districts, researchers found relationships (albeit weak) between strategic planning and student achievement in reading, language arts, and mathematics at several grade levels (Basham & Lunenburg, 1989). Armstrong's (1982) review of fifteen studies discovered that only five resulted in a statistically significant relationship between formal planning and improved performance. Similarly, a study conducted by Zook and Allen (2001) examined the profitability of more than 1,800 companies and found that seven out of eight companies failed to achieve lucrative increases even though 90 percent of the companies had detailed strategic plans with targets of much higher growth.

These findings indicate how difficult it is to determine the relationship between planning and performance (achievement), and also reveal the limited relationship between strategic planning and deep implementation (Kaplan & Norton, 2005). Mintzberg (1994) concludes, "Strategic planning is not strategic thinking. Indeed, strategic planning often spoils strategic thinking . . . the most successful strategies are visions, not plans" (p. 107).

Some studies have suggested that formal planning can lead to inflexible and myopic practices, or simply waste time and important resources (Bryson & Roering, 1987; Halachmi, 1986; Mintzberg, 1994). The speculation that planning has little value is supported by a Kentucky study that found that the most common, elaborate forms of improvement planning have a *negative* relationship to achievement (Kannapel & Clements, 2005). Moreover, Pfeffer and Sutton (2000) suggest that "formal planning is essentially unrelated to organizational performance" (p. 43).

It is still not unusual to find lengthy one hundred–page plans that spend more time describing the history of the school and its facility than planned changes in educational practice. The use of multipage planning templates and compliance with numerous requirements imposed by governing agencies promote "overload, fragmentation, and a lack of coherence" (Fullan, 1999, p. 27), elements Fullan describes as enemies of improvement. Elmore (2000) warns that planning and its related professional development simply ensure "lots of change, but not much improvement" (p. 12). Schmoker (2006), reflecting on formal Department of Education planning documents, concludes, "These templates precluded focused effort" (p. 35). In Title I middle schools in Illinois, school improvement planning was narrowly targeted on test results and was fragmented as a schoolwide endeavor (Cepela, 2008). Reeves' (2002a) personal observations of the strategic planning process as well as interviews with individuals involved in the process caution us that while there is "potential for clarity and cohesiveness," there is "potential for chaos and exhaustion" as well (p. 105).

The meta-analysis of effective leadership practices conducted by Marzano, Waters, and McNulty (2005) identifies quantifiable indicators of leadership that were related to school improvement, including the importance of establishing clear goals, designing and implementing decisions, and monitoring the effectiveness of school practices. In other words, school leadership has a substantial effect on student achievement by facilitating school improvement processes; developing a shared vision; establishing concrete goals for curriculum, instruction, and assessment; and monitoring the effectiveness and their impact on student learning—in short, by planning.

Two studies found a strong and consistent association between quality school planning and overall student performance. Springboard Schools (2006) focused on three California school districts that each served at least two thousand students, of whom 39 percent or more received free or reduced lunch and 15 percent or more were English language learners. Districts were then sorted on the basis of students rated proficient or above on California math and English assessments. One of the districts, Elk Grove Unified School District, cited their planning process as being instrumental in closing achievement gaps for student subgroups. Each school in the district specified strategies to be implemented; in particular,

> these school site plans have gone from being dust catchers to one of the key mechanisms for capturing agreements about the strategies that the school will use to make progress toward the school's goals. Site-level teams meet with district staff several times a year to review progress on implementation of these plans. During these sessions, the teams focus on both progress and needs. These meetings conclude by identifying steps for the site-level team to take. (Springboard Schools, 2006, p. 52)

Similarly, Fernandez (2006) studied 309 public schools in Clark County School District (CCSD) in Nevada from 2005 through 2006. His study analyzed data from three sources: (1) a content analysis of each school's improvement plan from the Leadership and Learning Center (formerly the Center for Performance Assessment); (2) CCSD data regarding student performance on standardized examinations; and (3) data on CCSD school demographics and resources.

This is an important study given the district's demographics. Clark County School District is the fifth-largest school district in the United States and comprises rural, suburban, and urban areas. In 2006, the school district had 326 schools with over 300,000 students from very diverse backgrounds. The school district was growing at a rate of approximately ten thousand new students each year, and demographically was already a very diverse school district. Clark County offered an extraordinary opportunity for educators and school leaders to learn about school improvement, and its findings are broadly applicable to urban, rural, and suburban schools with similar demographics. Essentially, Fernandez (2006, p. 9) concludes that school improvement plan quality is "positively and significantly related to school performance. This holds true even when controlling for various other factors, or whether one uses various measures of school performance."

Systemic Applications

The approaches to improving schools worldwide are remarkably similar. In the United States, Ohio developed a comprehensive and ambitious effort to improve schools, characterized by a decision framework for leadership development and an accompanying electronic data analysis structure. Ohio's decision framework describes protocols for six major elements:

1. Data and decision making
2. Focused goal setting
3. Instruction and learning

4. Community engagement

5. Resource management

6. Building governance (personal communication with Cyndi Yoder, October 23, 2008)

These elements are designed to ensure a guaranteed and viable curriculum, align staffing decisions and personnel appraisals to school improvement efforts, establish teacher-led data teams and professional learning communities, and ensure deep implementation. Ohio has an extensive system of technical assistance and electronic support for school improvement, but the building blocks of the decision framework describe the broad components of school improvement.

Other states identify similar components. Washington encouraged schools to complete their improvement plans by adhering to eight stages of school improvement:

1. Assess readiness to benefit.

2. Collect, sort, and select data.

3. Build and analyze the school portfolio.

4. Set and prioritize goals.

5. Research and select effective practices.

6. Craft action plan.

7. Monitor implementation of the plan.

8. Evaluate impact on student achievement (Bergeson & Heuschel, 2005).

Tennessee distilled its school improvement effort into six major components:

1. School profile and collaborative process

2. Beliefs, mission, and vision

3. Academic and non-academic data analysis

4. Curricular, instructional, assessment, and organizational effectiveness

5. Action plan development

6. School improvement plan and process evaluation (Seivers, 2007)

Like Ohio and Washington, Tennessee gathers data, analyzes both student achievement and teaching practices, delineates the action plan (strategies, timelines, responsibilities, support systems), and evaluates the entire process.

Illinois approaches school improvement in terms of ten major components:

1. AYP performance targets

2. District information

3. Data/information collection

4. Data analysis

5. Action plan

6. Professional development

7. Learning standards implementation

8. Family/community involvement

9. Support systems

10. Review, monitoring, and revision (Koch, 2009)

The Illinois process again emphasizes similar aspects, echoing Washington's emphasis on monitoring and adding a professional development component.

This high degree of commonality among school improvement planning processes is evident outside of the United States as well. In Canada, the following attributes of quality school improvement planning were identified as a result of a comprehensive analysis of British Columbia schools:

▶ Focus on learning

▶ Analysis of data

▶ Inquiry and reflection

▶ Common instructional strategies

▶ Continued professional learning

▶ Meaningful collaboration

▶ Distributed leadership

▶ Family/community context (Lewis, 2006)

Like Tennessee and Ohio, British Columbia emphasized collaboration, adding distributed leadership and inquiry. Ontario developed a similar framework with the following components advanced as essential to school improvement efforts (developed in concert with the Leadership and Learning Center):

▶ A comprehensive needs assessment is implemented.

▶ SMART goals focus on what students should be able to do (limited in number)

▶ Research-based strategies are implemented to achieve the goal (no more than five to ten).

▶ Required resources are identified.

▶ Professional learning needs are addressed.

▶ Strategies to engage parents are identified.

▶ Monitoring strategies describe timelines, those responsible, and progress measures.

▶ Evaluation related to the overall plan is scheduled in order to determine next steps, midcourse corrections, and lessons learned. (Mattingley, 2008)

In the United Kingdom, as in the United States, school improvement has been characterized by three phases and seven steps (see table 1.4).

Table 1.4: United Kingdom's School Improvement Process

Prepare and engage	Create a planning process based on a shared vision of where you are now, what you want to accomplish and a clear idea of how the framework can help.
Identify objectives	Inside the classroom: set objectives for improving teaching and learning that consider standards of achievement and pupil well-being.
	Learning potential: reach a common understanding of the factors that affect pupils' learning potential and identify ways to help all pupils achieve to the best of their ability.
	Beyond the classroom: identify ways to improve the well-being of all pupils in the school and community through extended services and other provision.
Ensure successful outcomes	Personalise: assess the needs of targeted pupils or cohorts in order to develop personalised interventions and demonstrate their impact.
	Develop and prioritise solutions: generate and prioritise solutions that will help meet school improvement objectives and define success.
	Plan delivery and evaluation: create a practical and achievable plan for implementing and evaluating agreed school improvement objectives.

Training and Development Agency for Schools, 2008

In Singapore, the School Excellence Model (Pak Tee, 2003) examines outcomes and processes (student learning and adult teaching and leading) to continuously question current practices and pursue new ways of thinking to achieve desired results. The components, such as alignment of assessments to professional practice and professional learning, are similar to those found in the United States, Canada, and the United Kingdom. In Singapore, the school improvement process is viewed as seamless links in a chain that is only as strong as its weakest element.

Each of these school improvement planning templates include common elements, such as data gathering and analysis; focused and prioritized goal setting; and strategies supported by professional development, monitoring, and evaluation. The Leadership and Learning Center developed a framework (2005b) to assess the quality of planning, implementation, monitoring, and evaluation that conforms to templates of most states, provinces, and education ministries. Figure 1.2 (page 20) illustrates the key component links in that improvement cycle.

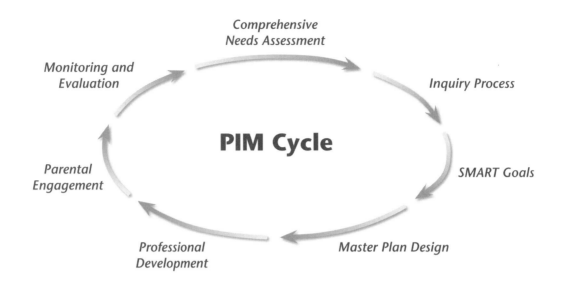

Figure 1.2: The framework for leadership in school improvement.

Leadership and Learning Center, 2005b

This process has been employed widely to analyze the quality of school improvement planning from Bermuda to Ontario to Pasadena. Lessons learned using this template have helped identify discrete best practices in school leadership that distinguish common practices today from best practices for tomorrow. The interaction of these steps provides a unique vantage point into school improvement and correlates teaching and leadership practices with improved achievement. School improvement, by definition, is designed to build capacity through professional practice and improve outcomes in terms of student achievement, and is most likely to occur when collaboration and accountability are evident and pervasive in the school culture.

Collaboration and Accountability: Cornerstones of School Improvement

The phases of planning, implementation, monitoring, and evaluation are essential to school improvement efforts, but any discussion of school improvement is incomplete without a review of research and best practices in terms of collaboration and accountability. Collaboration and accountability represent the cornerstones of school improvement because collaboration ensures that collective wisdom informs each component, and accountability ensures that transparency, defined responsibilities, and follow-through occur for each component.

In many ways, the design and development of professional learning communities (DuFour, DuFour, & Eaker, 2008; Hord, 1997) are also the design and development of effective school improvement efforts. DuFour, DuFour, and Eaker (2006) delineate four critical questions that drive the work of professional learning communities:

1. What do we want each student to learn?

2. How will we know when each student has learned it?

3. How will we respond when a student experiences difficulty in learning?

4. How will we respond when a student already knows it? (p. 2)

Together, these questions invite teams of teachers to examine and modify curriculum (question 1), assessment (question 2), and instruction (questions 3 and 4). The premise of professional learning communities is that teacher teams are the most efficient and effective means of managing and improving all three components of effective teaching. Professional learning communities engage teacher teams around the work of school improvement.

Shirley Hord (1997) identifies five attributes of professional learning communities: (1) shared values and vision, (2) collective learning and application, (3) supportive and shared leadership, (4) supportive conditions, and (5) shared personal practice. Each of these aspects describes the kinds of changes needed to ensure school improvement efforts are implemented deeply schoolwide or systemwide. For example, professional learning communities are designed to prioritize needs based on shared values, and to craft interventions that chart a path to preferred practice and success. *Collaboration* is, in fact, the forum for effective decision making (White, 2005a). Even directives to establish a common understanding of expectations are rarely implemented outside of a collaborative meeting. Collaboration provides the incubator for innovation, synergy, and improved ideas (Surowiecki, 2004). The power of collaboration has been borne out dramatically in the research (DuFour et al., 2005; Goddard, Goddard, & Tschannen-Moran, 2007; Surowiecki, 2004).

Accountability conjures up stories about "carrots and sticks," and research reveals that gains in student achievement have been considerable since the advent of No Child Left Behind (School Library Journal, 2008). However, sustaining gains requires much more than taking responsibility for results. Hanushek and Raymond (2005) found that though accountability improves scores of all students, there is no significant difference between accountability measures that simply report scores and those that attach consequences. Accountability works, but how we approach accountability makes a difference. Doug Reeves, in *Accountability in Action* (2004b), views accountability as a continuous improvement cycle with structures that encourage open and transparent communication; clarity of expectations; and a focus on solid, long-term results and values. A refreshing element of Reeves' framework is an emphasis on accountability for all, regardless of whether you are the chairman of the board, superintendent of schools, building custodian, kindergarten teacher, or a third-grade student. Consequently, the type of accountability that distinguishes next-generation school improvement plans from first-generation plans reflects *inclusive* practices or accountability for all rather than *exclusive* practices or accountability for some, which seems to typify most first-generation improvement plans. In other words, next-generation school improvement plans will not only monitor and measure the students' results (such as scores on large-scale tests, districtwide assessments, and classroom formative assessments), but also the effectiveness of practices adults perform throughout the system (such as instruction, assessment, and leadership) as well as the relationship between the two. Organizations that monitor and measure both adult actions and the effect those actions have on student performance will be poised to replicate the most effective strategies and discard those that are unrelated to improved achievement.

Taking Stock

Effective and transformative school improvement is less about what is being fixed and more about how the fixes will take place. Improvement, as opposed to mere change, will require a new paradigm that disrupts the status quo enough to engage professionals in developing, refining, and sustaining practices to improve achievement. After a generation of school improvement efforts— even well-intentioned, thoughtful improvement plans authored by well-meaning and capable individuals—most schools and districts still struggle to raise student performance. Our premise is simple: attention to the details of planning, implementation, monitoring, and evaluation is key to real and lasting school improvement. Carefully examining these details reveals best practices, as well as a path forward, and allows the early promise of school improvement to realize its potential. School improvement must enhance student achievement, but efforts that focus on achievement to the exclusion of capacity building and improved professional practice rarely produce the desired achievement. There are amazing examples of best practices in schools, but they are far from common. *School Improvement for the Next Generation* is a search to better understand school improvement phases and formalize emerging leadership practices into a user-friendly model for an uncertain future.

Final Thoughts

Despite enormous policy, programmatic, and financial investments in school improvement, results have been limited at best. The cumulative efforts of school improvement have produced very minimal gains even after almost four decades (Gonzalez et al., 2004; Grigg et al., 2006).

School improvement has taken many twists and turns to increase student achievement since the early 1980s by focusing on curriculum and classroom interventions, the impact of leadership on teaching and learning, the school as the unit of improvement, and a systems approach that acknowledges the impact of central office actions on school improvement as well as school-level efforts on the central office.

The systems approach represents an evolution in school improvement thinking that has helped educators view school improvement as a seamless process with each link in the chain strengthening the overall effort and supporting the next phase. Like our physicist, educators approached each of the fixes by relying on detailed, rational, and strategic improvement plans that project gains over long spans of time rather than focusing on short-term gains. Practitioners all too often make school improvement planning decisions that are so accepted and widely recommended that they are rarely questioned—yet are deeply flawed (Pfeffer & Sutton, 2006).

Many of the practices Byron initiated are best practices that will be addressed in further detail. Other practices from KCHS that represent the limits of the first generation of school improvement efforts will be reviewed as well. Throughout, we encourage readers to record their hunches, trials, and successes, to learn from their mistakes, and to make sure that each school improvement cycle learns from the previous one. We believe you will find that *School Improvement for the Next Generation* describes practical applications the next generation of leaders will need in order to close not only existing achievement gaps, but the knowing-doing gap (Pfeffer & Sutton, 2000) as well.

Key Questions for Team Study

Improvement means change in practice.
What is the premise behind this statement? How does it apply to the improvement plans generated by your school or district?

Success is best sustained when goals are few.
Why might that be the case? What advantage do schools and districts with few goals have over schools and districts with many?

Describe possible indicators you might use to determine whether your plan has too many or too few goals or action steps.

A leader's daily discipline determines successful implementation.
What message did Byron send to his staff about the importance of school improvement? What was needed to ensure better implementation across departments?

The promise of school improvement holds great potential for reform.
To what degree have lessons from school improvement been applied to reform your practices and inform the culture of your school or school system?

2 ▶ Making Improvements That Matter

The pathology of American schools is that they know how to change. They know how to change promiscuously and at the drop of a hat. What schools do not know how to do is to improve, to engage in sustained and continuous progress toward a performance goal over time.

—*Richard Elmore*

SEPTEMBER 18, 3:00 P.M. The school improvement leadership team was made up of extraordinary educators, and the September update was a celebration of a focused effort across KCHS to implement each item on the action plan: increasing the emphasis on explaining reasoning in mathematics; making activities, remediation, and mentoring as accessible and inclusive as possible for the entire student body; and advancing the rigor, thinking, and quality of academic performance in reading and language arts, especially for at-risk students. Everything appeared to be on track. Driven by the data from table 1.1 (page 7), Kelly County High School's thirty-first annual school improvement plan was beginning to take shape with developed goals for math, reading/language arts, and student well-being.

For twenty-one years, especially with the health and physical education and career and tech departments, Byron had struggled to engage some teachers to implement anything schoolwide. When initiatives were developed by his school improvement leaders, however, colleagues were much more willing to implement those changes than anything that appeared to be an order from administration.

This year, Byron had his school improvement leadership team develop a template with key phases of school improvement that would provide a common understanding and language, regardless of goals or activities. The plan for addressing reading/language arts is depicted in table 2.1. Goals for math and student well-being used the same template. Byron was certain that this new template would help his faculty embrace the school improvement process, and he wanted everyone to review and sign off on it before moving to the next step. After just a few moments, the leadership team gave its stamp of approval, and the entire meeting was used to analyze the data and draw inferences regarding what worked and why.

Once the school year was in progress, however, the goals proved difficult to implement. In October, Helen, as English department chair, was called in to help select curriculum mapping software, which caused her to miss two afternoons a week as well as the late-start Wednesday when she would otherwise be assisting KCHS staff. Byron was under a lot of pressure to be more visible for the football team, which was now 7–1 and had a very good chance to win the state title for the first time in thirty-four years, and the booster club asked for five minutes at the October staff meeting that became fifteen, eliminating the school improvement update.

Table 2.1: KCHS English/Language Arts School Improvement Plan—Goal 1

Needs Assessment: Sixteen of thirty-two subgroups failed to make adequate yearly progress. In particular, students with individual education plans (IEPs), students eligible for free or reduced lunch (FRL), and African American boys did not meet the standard.	
Inquiry Process Results	
Causal Factors—What Didn't Work?	**Causal Factors—What Is Working?**
General and special education teachers lacked structured planning time.	Daily critical thinking activities aligned to each curriculum have been incorporated.
There was limited emphasis at all ability levels on higher-order thinking skills that allow students to apply strategies to comprehend, interpret, and evaluate informational text.	Administrators and staff members in each department participate in a scheduled review of classroom walkthroughs.
Reading strategies were used inconsistently in all content areas.	Some teachers implement High School Performance Assessment (HSPA) warm-up drills that incorporate revising and editing skills, open-ended response, and literary terms.
Proficiency tutorial programs lacked participation by IEP students.	Some teachers use the Advanced Placement (AP) syllabus and AP required textbook to increase rigor in the classroom, administer timed writings every three weeks, and measure performance with the AP rubric.

Goal 1: Students at KCHS will show increased achievement in reading on the spring 2012 HSPA. Specific improvement will be made by the IEP subgroup in all reading areas and performance strands (such as comprehension, literary analysis, and vocabulary).

Strategy/ Action Plan	Formative/ Summative Measurement	Responsible Person	Resources Needed	Timeline
Teachers will implement HSPA warm-up drills that incorporate revising and editing skills, open-ended response, and literary terms in lessons.	Benchmark test data Common assessments Classroom walkthroughs	Teachers English/language arts coordinator Department chairs	Released HSPA items Campus online HSPA Warm-Ups book: HPSA coach Jumpstart HPSA Roadmap to HSPA	September 2011– February 2012
Teachers will use the AP syllabus and AP textbook to increase rigor in the classroom.	Data from timed writings, rubrics, and free writes The AP rubric will measure performance	Pre-AP teachers and AP teachers	Released HSPA test HSPA coach Jumpstart HSPA Roadmap to HSPA AP rubric	Third week of grading cycle Timed writings every three weeks
All departments will establish a reading initiative.	Collect reading initiatives—all departments Review lesson plans	Teachers Department chairs	Sample district reading initiatives Teacher resources on higher levels of Bloom's Taxonomy	Department meetings each month August to December
Monitoring and evaluation will occur.	KCHS interim fall/ spring English/ language arts assessments English department common assessments HSPA spring results	English department Learning improvement team Principals		Quarterly: October January March May

Protecting What Matters

Change, as Richard Elmore describes in the epigraph, is the easy part; schools "know how to change promiscuously and at the drop of a hat." What is much more difficult is protecting what should not be changed. The most effective school improvement efforts protect the focus and integrity of their plan by straining every request through that filter. Despite some admirable efforts, many of KCHS's planned improvements failed to get off the ground because of a variety of interruptions, unanticipated events, and a general leadership failure to protect what matters. Because the principal failed to recognize and protect the most vital aspects of school improvement, the impact of even the best practices was compromised. What is most important about school improvement? What should be protected?

We learned in chapter 1 that the basic components that define school improvement are markedly similar regardless of state, province, rural, or urban environment, and the basic format for improving schools consistently reflects some form of a continuous improvement cycle. To succeed in making lasting, meaningful improvements, the school improvement framework must focus on six phases: collaboration, accountability, planning, implementation, monitoring, and evaluation. The leadership practices that support this framework must be protected, deepened, and facilitated. The way those phases are designed, connected, and executed determines the degree of success schools experience. Unfortunately, the school improvement process is rarely protected. Leaders like our KCHS principal are far too ready to allow traditional practices to interfere and interrupt, and Byron, talented and experienced as he is, struggles to see the forest for the trees.

Formalizing Best Practices

Lynch and Marrs (2009) suggest that the first generation of innovation creates a framework of solutions, strategies, and structures. The next generation of school improvement will both formalize proven best practices and increase the precision of the strategies provided by the first generation.

The authors have seen this process play out in terms of curriculum (Tomlinson et al., 2002; Wiggins & McTighe, 2005), assessment (Ainsworth & Viegut, 2006; Guskey, 2007; Popham, 2003, 2008), and instruction (Anderson & Krathwohl, 2001; Heacox, 2002; Hill & Flynn, 2006; Marzano, 2007; Marzano, Pickering, & Pollock, 2001; Schmoker, 2004; Wenglinsky, 2002). Each time, the first generation of reform established a framework of solutions and structures that would later be replaced by a defined set of best practices. For example, from the effective schools movement emerged Madeline Hunter's lesson design (1982) and Larry Lezotte's seven Correlates of Effective Schools (2008), structures that defined the movement and best practices. The best example may be the seminal meta-analysis work conducted by Marzano et al. (2001) that distilled many of the most effective instructional strategies into nine discrete categories of proven best practices. This framework has assisted teachers in applying the research of a generation through a defined set of best practices.

It is established that effective professional learning communities (DuFour et al., 2005) increase student achievement. Accountability, standards, common formative assessments, and data-driven decision making (Reeves, 2006) are also well-established essential practices that promote gains in student achievement.

Understanding which attributes of school improvement are associated with increased achievement can help leaders protect what matters. The next-generation framework distinguishes common practices in school improvement from uncommon practices that future learners and leaders will need. Table 2.2 compares first-generation practices that have brought us this far and next-generation practices that are formalized and employed at proficient or higher levels to yield sustained gains in achievement and growth in terms of organizational capacity. For example, the first generation insisted on measurable goal statements, while the next generation describes precise, targeted goals in terms of both content outcomes and growth for targeted groups of students.

Table 2.2: First- Versus Next-Generation School Improvement Practices

	First Generation of School Improvement	Next Generation of School Improvement
Collaboration	For compliance and completion	For action research and improvement
Accountability	For students (exclusive)	For students and adults (inclusive)
Planning	Assumptions are unrealistic. A needs assessment "silos" unprioritized student achievement, attendance, and behavior data. Only student achievement (effect) data are analyzed. Goals are vague and numerous.	Assumptions are evidence based. A needs assessment "funnels" and prioritizes student achievement, instructional, and leadership data. Instruction and leadership practice (cause) data as well as student achievement (effect) data are analyzed. Analysis rules out inconclusive data and rules in patterns and trends. SMART goals are limited in number.
Implementation	Action steps are too numerous to implement well. Implementation is uneven. Strategies are research based. Action steps resemble a task analysis or are stated as student outcomes. Implementation by professionals is assumed. There is a menu of professional development options. Everyone is responsible, yet no one is in charge. Parents are involved in school activities.	A limited number of action steps are implemented well. Implementation is sustained and progressive. Strategies are both research based and targeted. Action steps are stated as observable, measurable adult practices. Implementation by professionals is guided (supported). Professional development is focused. Champions of initiatives are responsible. Parents are engaged in targeted student achievement and have access and training.
Monitoring	Completion of steps is infrequently monitored and measured, and findings are not acted upon. Educator participation is checked for compliance.	Completion of steps is frequently monitored and measured, and findings are acted upon. Fidelity of implementation informs adult practice. Monitoring data are used to make midcourse corrections and provide feedback.
Evaluation	Evaluations rarely occur. Student results are reported. Lessons that resulted from the improvement process are not used.	Evaluations are ongoing. Evaluations analyze and report both student (effect) and adult (cause) results. Lessons learned are systemically and systematically identified and applied to the next improvement cycle.

The next-generation school improvement process is sequential, and begins with the planning phase, which includes (1) a broad illumination of the school's strengths and weaknesses, (2) a comprehensive needs assessment, and (3) a winnowing or systematic elimination of irrelevant data so that the school can spotlight the most critical areas of need on which to collectively focus its improvement efforts. This process results in SMART goals that are then addressed through a limited number of measurable steps and strategies, acted upon during the implementation phase, monitored frequently, and then evaluated at the end of the cycle—at which point the whole process begins again.

Lessons From the Field

We developed the next-generation framework after an empirical review of school improvement plans. Our review began during work with Clark County School District (CCSD) in Las Vegas, Nevada, the United States' fifth-largest urban school system. Figure 2.1 depicts the achievement gains of this district from 2004 to 2008, the early years of No Child Left Behind.

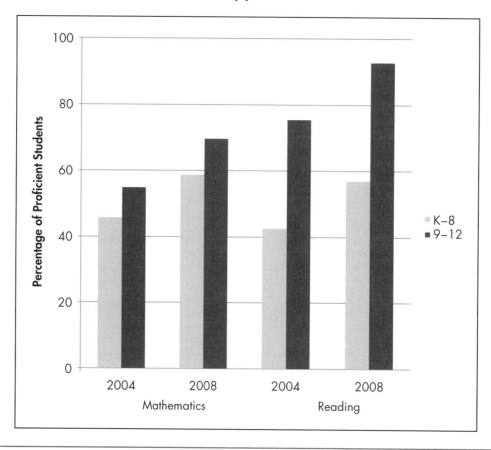

Figure 2.1: Clark County School District reading and math gains on the CRT and HSPE, 2004–2008.

Reeves et al., 2007, used with permission

Clark County School District showed significant student achievement gains in reading and mathematics, despite low funding, limited tenure for administrators in the same building, almost eighty thousand English language learners (ELLs), and a highly mobile student and faculty.

Through our work with Clark County, we analyzed almost one thousand school improvement plans from throughout the district over a three-year period and found some remarkable relationships between engaging in school improvement phases and gains in student achievement. Figure 2.2 compares the results of schools demonstrating proficiency in emerging best practices in school improvement with schools relying on traditional approaches to this complex work. Increases represent achievement gains on the Nevada CRT (criterion-referenced test) assessment grades K–8, and the High School Performance Examination (HSPE). Actual percent gains are displayed in table 2.3 (page 32).

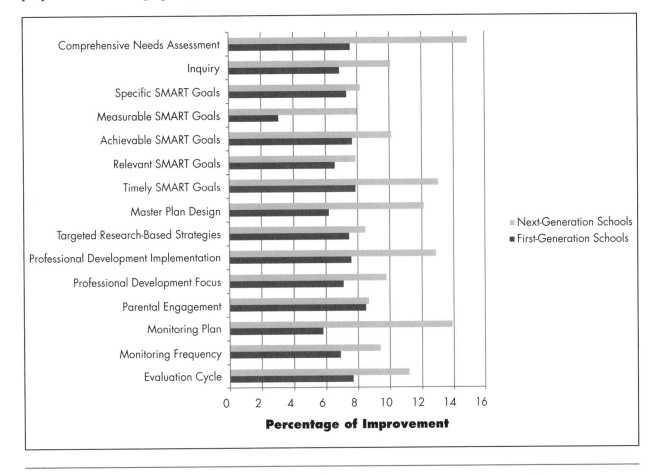

Figure 2.2: Clark County School District achievement gains on the CRT and HSPE as a result of school improvement, 2004–2007.

Reeves et al., 2007, used with permission

Table 2.3: Actual Percentage Gains for the Comparison in Figure 2.2

School Improvement Phases	Proficient	Needs Improvement	School Improvement Phases	Proficient	Needs Improvement
Comprehensive Needs Assessment	14.9%	7.6%	Targeted Research-Based Strategies	8.50%	7.45%
Inquiry	10.10%	6.90%	Professional Development Focus	9.80%	7.10%
Specific SMART Goals	8.20%	7.35%	Professional Development Implementation	12.9%	7.6%
Measurable SMART Goals	8.0%	3.1%	Parental Engagement	8.70%	8.50%
Achievable SMART Goals	10.15%	7.70%	Monitoring Plan	13.9%	5.8%
Relevant SMART Goals	7.90%	6.60%	Monitoring Frequency	9.4%	6.9%
Timely SMART Goals	13.1%	7.9%	Evaluation Cycle	11.2%	7.7%
Master Plan Design	12.1%	6.2%			

Reeves et al., 2007

School, regional, and district plans in CCSD that met next-generation criteria for exemplary school improvement demonstrated greater achievement gains than school plans scored as needing improvement. In monitoring, comprehensive needs assessment, and master plan design, the differences were dramatic, and in others (such as parental engagement), the distinctions were minimal. The CCSD experience was significant because success on every single school improvement step was predictive of higher achievement gains for more than nine hundred schools over a three-year period. Results provided a compelling rationale to pay much closer attention to the relationship between school improvement components and student achievement results, because small changes can have large effects.

Clark County School District helped us learn that best practices in school improvement were just as meaningful to student achievement as best classroom practices in curriculum, assessment, and instruction. Similar findings across the continent are referenced in later chapters. For too long, school improvement plans have had no "shelf life" (Marx, 2006, p. 3)—plans are compliantly developed, filed in three-ring binders, and then placed on a shelf to gather dust. Marx urges educators to make certain their improvement plan moves from the "top shelf to the top of the desk and become[s] an ongoing agenda" (p. 3). This agenda should not only shape and inform day-to-day actions that inspire participants to achieve high levels of commitment, but should also identify improvement practices that are predictive of student achievement gains.

The distinguishing leadership practices in CCSD began our pursuit to define characteristics for the next generation of school improvement efforts. Now let's review an overview of key phases: collaboration, accountability, planning, implementation, monitoring, and evaluation.

Collaboration

School improvement is a quintessential collaborative process that compels school teams to continually grow their instructional and leadership capacity schoolwide, thereby improving student achievement classroom by classroom, grade level by grade level, and department by department. It does not and cannot occur in isolation. An element that distinguishes next-generation efforts from first-generation efforts is recognizing that a focused set of schoolwide initiatives that center on the common good are much more effective than fragmented efforts that are determined in isolation at the individual grade or department level (Garcia, 2006; Surowiecki, 2004). Collaboration provides the opportunity for collective decisions and collective wisdom to prevail (Goddard, Hoy, & Hoy, 2000). School improvement can neither improve achievement nor build capacity without collective wisdom applied to collective decisions that advance needed change. Collaboration is perhaps the greatest strength of current school improvement efforts, and the next generation will only build on that foundation.

Accountability

Accountability is synonymous with school improvement, as the best aspects of accountability lead to improved performance. Reeves (2004b) views accountability as a series of actions and structures that focuses on student achievement through congruence (alignment of effort), respect for diversity (differences in students, context, curricula, and culture), accuracy (correct measures used appropriately), specificity (focus on adult practices as well as test scores), feedback for continuous improvement, universality (holding all stakeholders accountable), and fairness (rules of the game are understood and consistently applied). Universality, or inclusive accountability, is particularly instructive in that it invites all participants in the process to ask for help, contribute ideas, and receive feedback. Reeves' model assumes that learning is the ultimate purpose of an accountability plan, regardless of the role or position of participants. Accountability is often characterized as "being responsible for results," a quality demonstrated when transparency and feedback are evident. Next-generation school improvement anticipates and embraces these key practices. Inclusive accountability and collaboration are the bookends of the next generation of school improvement; they also apply to each school improvement phase to better define best practice.

Planning

Planning, which is discussed in chapter 3 in more detail, is the foundation for improvement. Successful leadership in next-generation school improvement planning consists of a comprehensive needs assessment (broadly examining how both students and adults in the system are performing), an inquiry process (data analysis, prioritization, and elimination), and development of SMART goals (see fig. 2.3, page 34).

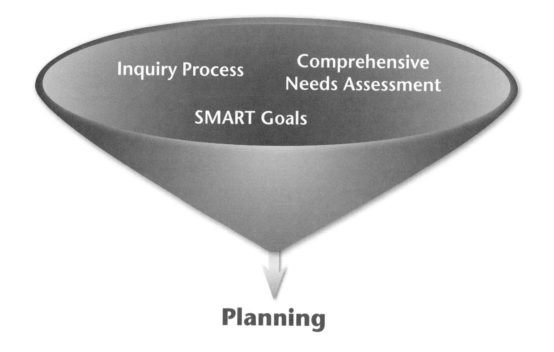

Planning

Figure 2.3: Steps of successful leadership in planning.

Comprehensive Needs Assessment

First-generation school improvement plans are typically awash in student achievement (effect) data and void of adult instruction (cause) data. School improvement teams need to understand that the critical task in the planning phase is to rule in the important data available to them while ruling out the inconsequential. In other words, the objective in a comprehensive needs assessment is "not to accumulate all of the data you can, but to 'can' (i.e., get rid of) most of the data you accumulate" (Wolcott, 1990, p. 35); otherwise, the scope of team efforts will be too large, and the opportunity to focus on high-leverage improvement opportunities will be lost.

Inquiry Process

Gathering data to determine areas of priority ensures that goals target the significant and few, rather than the trivial and many (Scholtes, 2001). School improvement processes typically include a needs assessment that addresses student result data followed by a goal-setting process, but few include a needs assessment that looks at both student and adult needs as a process of inquiry that winnows the data to the vital areas. The inquiry process is essential because it ensures that needs-assessment data are connected and purposeful in generating novel hypotheses (IF/THEN statements) based on the context of teaching and learning at a specific school. That is, the inquiry process analyzes data to yield priorities that represent high-leverage targets of improvement opportunity in student needs and professional practice, and the resulting hypotheses guide improvement teams to articulate SMART goals. First-generation efforts, lacking a comprehensive assessment of needs, typically defer to faculty preferences or a repeat of the same goals or processes as used in previous improvement efforts. The lack of a quality process of inquiry also hinders the development of SMART goals. Without a systematic process to narrow the focus and develop meaningful hypotheses for action, goals tend to be selected without the insight necessary to link them to the most effective strategies and supports.

SMART Goal Setting

First-generation planning often culminates in articulating goals that are based more on subject content than on practices. School improvement plans commonly outline separate goals for reading, mathematics, science, and wellness or student behavior. Each is treated as a separate, linear project, and goals tend to be generic to the entire school population and only rarely ascribe to close achievement gaps. Mike Schmoker (1999) remarks that setting academic goals for the school as a whole does have a powerful, coalescing effect on teachers and administrators: "Goals and the commitment that they generate are the glue that holds teams together" (p. 24). For goals to hold teams together, however, they need to be limited in number, stated in specific terms, and measurable; otherwise the goals will not be as effective as they could be.

Implementation

The implementation phase of first-generation school improvement typically includes action steps that describe program initiatives, list things to do (reminiscent of a task analysis), express student outcome goals, offer a range of professional development, suggest broad timeline spans, list groups of individuals responsible for various sections of the plan, and limit parent involvement to attendance at school functions. The major shortcoming of these efforts, however, is that it is assumed each action step will be implemented fully and that staff are proficient at delivering the outcomes.

Next-generation implementation efforts are much more explicit and precise. Figure 2.4 depicts the five steps of implementation.

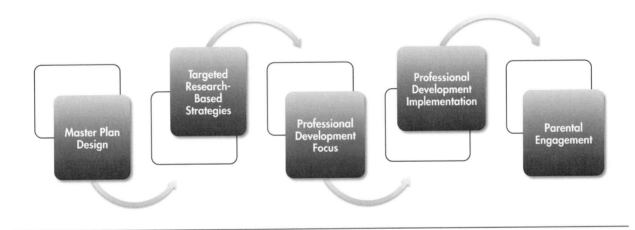

Figure 2.4: Steps of successful leadership in implementation.

Master Plan Design

In the next generation of school improvement, implementation follows a concise master plan that includes a limited number of measurable adult action steps; a description of how strategies will be implemented and coordinated; and a timeline of events. The timeline sets a schedule for:

▶ Introducing changes

▶ Establishing them in practice

▶ Monitoring them for fidelity of implementation against a standard of expected performance

▶ Providing opportunities for midcourse corrections when needed

Targeted Research-Based Strategies

Execution begins with implementation of targeted strategies—grounded in sound research in effective classroom and school practices—that are designed to address the learning needs of the underperforming student subgroups. In other words, it is not enough to choose a general high-yield instructional strategy; specific instructional strategies that lead to the most rapid rate of growth for *targeted student subgroups* must be selected. Toward that end, targeted research-based strategies take into consideration the context of learning (for the group of students most in need of intervention) and augment best practices with a protocol based on the needs of students at the local school.

Professional Development and Parental Engagement

Next-generation strategies always engage students by responding to the learning conditions and experiences of local classrooms and schools. Professional development is approached to ensure both focus and deep implementation, and parental engagement describes creative and empowering ways to include parents in the important work of improving learning in targeted areas of student achievement.

The five steps of implementation, which will be examined in detail in chapter 4, are inextricably linked. The finest professional development will have a weakened impact if it is competing with a number of complex and unrelated training efforts. Similarly, selection of a very powerful instructional strategy such as reciprocal teaching will have a weakened impact on achievement if it is not augmented with a local context for specific subgroups of learners. Each step is a link in the chain of excellence in school improvement, and the finest selection of strategies absent efforts to sustain professional development will produce an outcome less than what would be otherwise possible.

Monitoring and Evaluation

While monitoring and evaluation are described in separate chapters in this volume, it is important to recognize that the two are interdependent. While a monitoring plan details how often professional educators charged with implementation receive feedback, the evaluation process ensures that teams learn lessons from each improvement cycle. Each improvement plan should be sufficiently precise to serve as action research in the field.

Figure 2.5 depicts how monitoring and evaluation combine in terms of both a sequence of events and a foundation for learning. Monitoring provides sufficient information to help teachers decide to either continue as planned or to modify the action steps. Monitoring exists primarily as a means of providing feedback to an improvement process that invites midcourse corrections. Evaluation is the foundation of the pyramid for two reasons: (1) evaluation is the cumulative and summative activity of next-generation school improvement efforts, and (2) evaluation represents the point where lessons learned inform next steps.

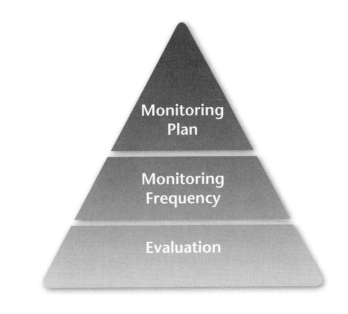

Figure 2.5: Steps of successful leadership in monitoring and evaluation.

The three layers of figure 2.5 are mutually interdependent, as evaluation is difficult unless informed by careful monitoring of growth and capacity indicators. Monitoring can inform practice in the short term, but unless the results of monitoring are examined in terms of the overall purpose and goals of the school improvement effort (evaluation), its benefit is limited to the current plan. Monitoring is about data gathering, while evaluation is about learning from that data. The quality of one informs the other.

Monitoring Plan

Monitoring is formative in that it provides a window into the current improvement efforts and offers feedback to teams and individual teachers about the quality of their implementation efforts to date. Monitoring is to school improvement what checking for understanding is to classroom instruction. It invites adjustments by describing explicit data, when that data will be gathered and reported, and who will be responsible for reporting progress. Without these critical components, monitoring will continue to serve as a compliance activity, rather than offer rich guidance and insight about teaching and learning and what is working and what is not.

A next-generation monitoring plan describes a continuous improvement cycle and provides an agile mechanism to respond to data monitored through midcourse corrections. Quality plans routinely examine results in both student achievement and professional practice by monitoring two forms of data: (1) the teaching and leadership practices that precede student results and specify the quality and fidelity of implementation of selected best practices and (2) the indicators of student achievement from a variety of perspectives, including student behavior, preparedness, and participation.

Monitoring Frequency

Monitoring frequently—at least five to ten times annually—allows teams to assess and respond to the need for adjustments in instruction and leadership support in order to deliver that instruction more effectively. While a number of studies recommend even more frequent assessments of student achievement (Marzano, 2007; Yeh, 2007), we recommend a level of frequency that provides frequent review and sufficient response time to change practices systematically.

Evaluation

While monitoring is a formative process, evaluation occurs within the improvement cycle (formative) *and* represents the final step in the improvement cycle (summative). Evaluation is the reflection-after-action part of the process that causes school teams to examine results, infer cause-and-effect relationships, recall specific examples to support their inferences, determine the degree to which improvement efforts worked, and more importantly, roll this identified collective learning into the next improvement cycle. This allows teams to weed out practices that fail to yield desired results and to replicate successes that do.

Evaluation ensures that each school compares planned outcomes with actual outcomes, identifies lessons learned, and applies those lessons to future plans. Next-generation evaluation is also transparent in that compared results (positive and negative), as well as plans to update future cycles, are systematically communicated to primary stakeholders (families, educators, staff, patrons, partners, and the public). Evaluation is part of a continuous improvement timeline—a yearlong calendar that identifies specific, coordinated dates for each of the steps of the school improvement cycle for *all* goals. Quality evaluation always explicitly describes the actions that will be taken in light of the evidence presented. Powerful evaluation plans respond to a series of hypotheses for action, first in the inquiry process and subsequently in the action plan components. As a result, schools and districts will have more complete information at their disposal to identify lessons from their efforts.

We have identified six common phases—collaboration, accountability, planning, implementation, monitoring, and evaluation—in school improvement planning, which the following chapters will expand on in greater detail, but the strategies and structures that will define the next generation of school improvement are drawn from ideas and solutions that champions of school improvement have applied in schools and systems across North America.

The Champions

The following schools and school districts have taught us much; their school improvement processes have resulted in a number of improvements in the components and cycle used to describe next-generation school improvement.

Clark County School District, Arlene Lewis, director of research and accountability. Clark County, as noted earlier, was the source of the Leadership and Learning Center's initial research findings about school improvement. The district continues to provide extensive analysis of school improvement. Steady and significant improvement for this large, urban district is clearly associated with their next-generation planning, implementation, and monitoring efforts; distributed leadership; and systematic celebration of student gains.

Elkhart Community Schools, John Hill, director of curriculum and instruction. Elkhart Community Schools, located in Elkhart, Indiana, pursued an aggressive staff development effort designed to equip all teachers and building leaders with the knowledge and skills they deemed necessary to customize their instruction to individual students. Toward that end, the district incorporated a number of highly successful implementation and monitoring strategies to improve or change their current practices and measure the resulting outcome. Two principals—Kristie Stutsman, principal at Westside Middle School, and Jean Creasbaum, principal at Osolo Elementary School—were singled out for their effective implementation of the district's professional development initiatives.

Greece School District, Steve Achronovich, superintendent. Greece School District, located in New York, pursued a process of establishing SMART (specific, measureable, achievable, relevant, timely) goals as the lever to improve capacity of faculty and increase student achievement at all levels. After establishing a few concrete process goals, each school was provided latitude in developing its own improvement effort based on a comprehensive needs assessment of teaching practices, leadership actions, and student achievement.

Hastings and Prince Edward District School Board, Jan Montgomery, superintendent of education. Hastings and Prince Edward, located on the northern shores of Lake Ontario, developed a bold approach to school improvement that prescribed a discrete process of inquiry and a powerful monitoring process to capture insights about cause-and-effect relationships between professional practice and student achievement gains.

Hawthorn School District #73, Sue Zook, superintendent. In this Vernon Hills, Illinois, district, Zook adopted a next-generation template for school improvement, district support, and a process to refine and revise school improvement efforts while pursuing ambitious goals. In so doing, the district refined its continuous improvement processes and made the process of inquiry, comprehensive needs assessment, midcourse corrections, and replication of best school improvement practices the pillars of improvement efforts for the next generation.

Hillsboro School District, Dawn Montgomery, executive director of school improvement. Montgomery and her colleagues have worked diligently in Hillsboro, Oregon, over the past four years to engineer into their school improvement process much needed improvements to a next-generation planning template, which collectively focuses their thinking on prioritized student achievement targets and the practices of teachers and leaders to continually advance learning and student achievement.

Metropolitan School District, Lisa Lantrip, assistant superintendent for elementary education. Lantrip and her colleagues (principals Judy Stegemann, Nicole Law, and John Taylor) at this award-winning school system in Indianapolis, Indiana, have pursued a comprehensive and collegial approach to school improvement leadership that engages entire leadership teams in a midyear school improvement review process that serves as a model of school improvement monitoring, evaluation, midcourse corrections, and targeted research-based strategies.

Final Thoughts

This chapter offered a theory of action for school improvement based on collaboration, accountability, planning, implementation, monitoring, and evaluation. This theory builds on the first generation of school improvement by identifying not only the key steps, but also the best practices within those steps that contribute to improved gains in student achievement.

Educators have established frameworks to ensure quality lesson planning and to deliver effective teaching practices in the classroom (Ainsworth & Viegut, 2006; Danielson & McGreal, 2000; Guskey, 2007; Lezotte, 1984; Marzano, 2007; Reeves, 2006; Wiggins & McTighe, 2005), as well as to ensure effective leadership practices in school districts and schools (Marzano, 2003; Reeves, 2009a). Now a comparable framework, such as next-generation school improvement, is needed to provide creative, strategic, and verified efforts that improve student achievement and build capacity of faculty and staff. Our thesis is based on field experience of schools and districts representing 1.5 million students. Our theory of action is simple: make school improvement the most important work at each school, and do everything necessary to make best practice common practice.

Protecting what matters is paying attention to the details of school improvement and to the tasks of building capacity and sustaining successful practices. The next generation of teachers and school leaders deserve nothing less.

Key Questions for Team Study

Planning is the building block for school improvement.
What is the premise behind this statement? How does it apply to the improvement plans generated by your school or district?

Implementation is ensuring what needs to get done gets done.
Describe acts of leadership in your school or district that can provide you that assurance. Where are the leverage points within your organization that move ideas into action?

Monitoring is formative leadership.
What is the premise behind this statement? To what degree do you agree and why?

Evaluation is summative leadership.
How is evaluation different from reporting student achievement results? Describe the ideal function of an effective evaluation framework for your school or district.

3　The Planning Process

P lans are nothing; planning is everything.

—Dwight D. Eisenhower

NOVEMBER 6, 3:00 P.M. Back at Kelly County High School, the school improvement team had finished planning and was ready to start implementation. For this faculty meeting, Mi Lai, Kim, and Helen presented the plan along with data from the High School Performance Assessment (see table 1.1, page 7). As he listened to Helen facilitate the meeting, Byron knew he would miss her unassuming leadership and unselfish devotion to tackle whatever challenge was before her. Helen had educational gravitas, and whether the task was breaking a logjam in negotiations or examining the district's latest initiative, she was an incredible asset to KCHS and to Byron as principal.

"As committed as we are to serving all kids and as successful as we have been with most," Helen began, "KCHS is not reaching as many kids as we need to. It's not just the HSPA scores; it's also that these same demographics can be used as predictors of dropouts, office referrals, and tardiness. We have some great ideas for math, such as explaining reasoning in every class, and great ideas for our well-being goal through a coordinated case-management approach, but I'm most excited about assisting every department to adopt one initiative in *reading* this year. As you know, Joanne—our district coordinator for English/language arts—has provided a wide range of reading initiatives in terms of higher-order thinking strategies that can be implemented across the curriculum—from band to pottery to strength and conditioning to lab science—so we have lots of opportunities to get it right for all of our students. Before Mi Lai and Kim help each department select an initiative, are there any questions about what is expected?"

There were the usual questions about the time required to introduce reading activities in high school, and Joanne, Helen, Mi Lai, and Kim gave assurances about their availability to assist. All in all, the mood was upbeat and the faculty responsive.

"Please revisit the status of your initiative at your next department meeting, and we will ask one or two departments to describe their plan at the November 13 meeting. Thanks for coming, and you are dismissed," said Helen. Byron loved to witness distributive leadership in action, and looked forward to discussing it with Yohannon in the months to come.

A Connected Planning Process

This chapter describes three overlooked, rushed, and underutilized building blocks of school improvement planning that have the potential to leverage limited resources, focus efforts, and increase student achievement: comprehensive needs assessment, inquiry, and SMART goals. The history of school improvement is characterized more by fits and starts than steady growth, as schools frequently start over each and every year with new goals, new areas of focus, and new strategies. KCHS did not plan for their process to be characterized by fits and starts, but Helen and her team presented only one aspect of the plan while mentioning separate math and wellness goals. Even though KCHS agreed that each department should apply higher-order thinking to reading strategies appropriate to their content, the change initiative was extensive, and the route was unfamiliar to content experts outside of the humanities.

KCHS, under the keen eye and leadership of Helen's team, offered a series of protocols and strategies to ensure deep implementation in a one-page action plan, or so they thought (table 2.1, pages 26–27). The school understood that support was needed from a literacy expert, and by enlisting Joanne from the district office, KCHS was intentional about building capacity. The KCHS plan included effective collaborative processes and distributed leadership. The strategies they selected also reflected sound pedagogy, explaining reasoning in mathematics and higher-order reading instruction across the curriculum. The problem was that the plan was disconnected and fragmented, and driven more by the tradition to have two academic goals and one affective goal than by any real evidence suggesting that three goals were better than two, or two better than one.

Bryk, Sebring, Kerbow, Rollow, and Easton (1998) suggest that the main problem is not the absence of innovation in schools, but rather the presence of too many disconnected, episodic, fragmented, superficially adorned projects. Even when goals are maintained for multiple cycles, improvement efforts rarely build upon the experience of prior years. Successful school improvement means that protocols, strategies, and systems are modified as those who implement the innovation become sufficiently knowledgeable and skilled in the improved practice to ensure better results in student achievement. The next generation will therefore require a comprehensive needs assessment that shows the big picture of student needs to allow for the creation of a focused, unified plan.

Comprehensive Needs Assessment

There is an old Chinese folktale about three blind men who encounter an elephant for the first time and attempt to learn about it by touch alone. The story goes something like this:

> As three blind men happened upon an elephant, each exclaimed aloud. "It is a large rough thing, wide and broad, like a rug," said the first, grasping an ear. The second, holding the trunk, said, "I have the real facts. It is a straight and hollow pipe." And the third, holding a front leg, said, "It is mighty and firm, like a pillar."

Translated to school improvement, each sees the organization's problems clearly, but none sees how their actions interact with or impact the other two. The story concludes by observing that, given the men's way of knowing, they will never know an elephant.

Educators struggle every day to make sense of school improvement data. Most touch only small parts of the information and come away with a narrow and fragmented understanding of what it means. Many first-generation school improvement efforts rightly insist on multiple sources of student achievement data and augment achievement information with information about student behavior. Some educators employ quality item analyses to reveal gaps in student learning, which teachers address by balancing and integrating when and how content is delivered. Teams may even hypothesize as to which teaching practice contributed to the gains or declines recorded. Unfortunately, as long as the only evidence we bring to the table is exclusive to students, discussions will at best be hunches that beg further analysis.

The KCHS plan was straightforward in recognizing the need to close achievement gaps (sixteen of thirty-two subgroups performed below standard), but there is no indication that data about teaching were even considered. The school did posit the contributing factors and agreed that reading strategies were inconsistent and that higher-order thinking skills were not currently emphasized. These activities represent a solid first-generation needs assessment, but they miss the opportunity to go deeper faster and more effectively. When educators gather data about teaching practices, teams are more apt to identify relationships between their actions and are able to interpret student performance with confidence and precision. Without the ability to triangulate data from multiple perspectives simultaneously, many of the meaningful relationships about the context of improvement remain hidden. Analysis tools (such as triangulation, Ishikawa "fishbone" diagram, affinity diagram, Pareto chart, or nominal group technique) are critical to the next generation of comprehensive needs assessments because teams fluent in using such tools will need to explore and analyze data from multiple perspectives.

Comprehensive needs assessment is more than a good idea. We found a dramatic difference in student achievement gains in Clark County (2004–2007) by contrasting school achievement gains with evidence of comprehensive needs assessment (evidence of learning, teaching, and leadership data) in school improvement plans (fig. 3.1, page 46).

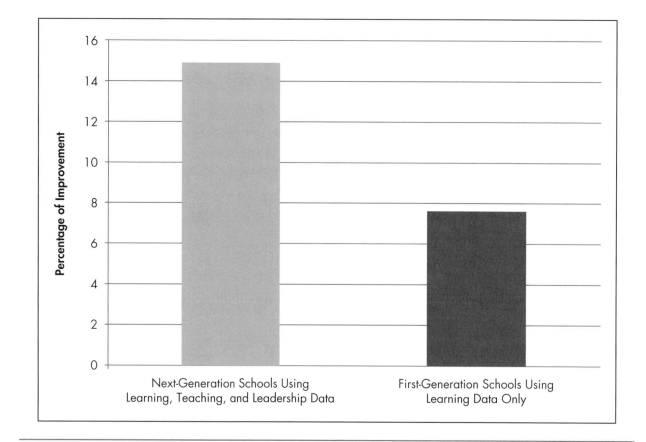

Figure 3.1: Clark County School District achievement gains on the CRT and HSPE as a result of comprehensive needs assessment, 2004–2007.

Reeves et al., 2007, used with permission

Which Data Are the Right Data?

Given dozens of possible sources of data available to each of us, how do we select the most meaningful and informative teaching or leadership data? How can we examine teaching data that range from greeting students at the door to grading practices to implementing a wide range of high-yield instructional strategies? Which antecedent practice is most valuable, and how does one know? The data we select determine the evidence that influences our assumptions and guides our decisions.

Types of Teaching and Leadership Data

Powerful instructional strategies are strong predictors of improved student achievement (Heacox, 2002; Hill & Flynn, 2006; Marzano, 2007). It is important to understand what an instructional strategy is: how a teacher arranges her room or assigns papers is not an instructional strategy. Four defining elements help distinguish an instructional strategy from a useful teacher routine, a classroom condition for learning, or even an administrative structure such as grading guidelines. Instructional strategies always:

1. Engage students in thinking

2. Involve established protocols for instructional delivery

3. Require professional development to acquire competence

4. Require practice with feedback to demonstrate mastery

Examples of strategies that engage thinking include provocative writing prompts, cogent use of metaphors and similes, multistep problems with the scientific method, or mathematical analysis of relationships in time and space. Protocols define the instructional strategy. Consider the following protocol for reciprocal teaching: (1) teachers guide students to *predict* what the reading selection is all about or what they expect to learn from the selection; (2) teachers introduce the reading, then invite students to *clarify* how the content differed from what was previously predicted; (3) following a first reading of the document or text, teachers invite the students to *question* and anticipate what might happen next, or what might have happened if events in the reading were changed or if the main character had made a different choice of action; and finally, (4) the teacher invites students to *summarize* the reading. Reciprocal teaching is thus defined by these four observable and measurable components: predict, clarify, question, and summarize.

In contrast, most agree differentiated instruction is a powerful instructional strategy, but unless it is defined more clearly (for example, it must include flexible grouping by interests, align with Bloom's Taxonomy, and appeal to multiple intelligences), it will not meet the test. If we know what an instructional strategy is, we also know what it is not, and we can measure its frequency, its quality, and the degree to which it is delivered.

School improvement teams can easily gather data on instructional strategies by inviting teachers to assess the degree to which they utilize them, as Karen Cencula did as principal of Townline Elementary in Hawthorn, Illinois. Karen simply invited her faculty to assess how often they engaged in specific strategies, teaching behaviors, and curriculum design efforts. The data enabled her improvement team to understand patterns and trends in student achievement and to recognize needed changes in their own practice that would otherwise have remained undiscovered.

The Hastings and Prince Edward District School Board in Ontario created a comprehensive and practical template to gather the right data to shape the right discussion. Table 3.1 (page 48) provides a snapshot of their comprehensive needs-assessment template. This template guides practitioners to collect data regarding strengths and successful practices that are already evident. It then has room for practitioners to document areas of concern, factors, and possible mitigating strategies. Superintendent Jan Montgomery remarks, "Working through the needs assessment challenged us to look beyond our student achievement data and have conversations that helped us reflect and think deeply about our strengths, challenges, and next steps. This provided the lens we needed to select an appropriate focus that was precise but would permeate many areas of instruction and student learning" (personal communication, January 16, 2009).

Table 3.1: Snapshot of Hastings and Prince Edward District Comprehensive Needs-Assessment Template, 2007

Areas of Strengths	Successful Practices	
Reading for meaning: Understanding explicitly stated information and ideas—63 percent proficient Some schools are showing overall improvement regardless of external supports (Turnaround/Ontario Focused Intervention Partnership [OFIP]); examples include Pinecrest, Tyendinaga, and Carswell. Turnaround Schools growth over three years has been very positive.	Data walls are in place in most schools. Highly effective literacy blocks are modeled in actual classrooms. Turnaround/OFIP strategies—such as use of data at professional learning community meetings, specific focus on running records to inform instruction, and consistent and frequent monitoring with feedback—are modeled. Creation of principal learning teams that focus on effective strategies has supported principals in understanding running records, greater sense of accountability, and culture of learning. Balanced literacy components have been the primary change in professional practice at Turnaround Schools in which gains have been sustained. Deep implementation sets the stage for extended implementation. Literacy partners in all schools are reported as impacting classroom practice positively. Agenda lists shared reading and alignment of professional development. Strategies for Success symposium provided practical ideas for 180 teachers. Team leaders report a greater focus resulting from PLC conversations.	
Areas of Concern	**Factors to Consider**	**Mitigating Strategies**

Making connections—57 percent proficient
 	
Larger school performance declined from 2006–2007; others had mixed results.
 	
Gender differences in reading and writing on the Educational Quality and Accountability Office (EQAO) reports were significant in 2008:
 	
Sixth-grade reading:
 	
   (Girls) 65 percent proficient
 	
   (Boys) 48 percent proficient
 	
Sixth-grade writing:
 	
   (Girls) 63 percent proficient
 	
   (Boys) 36 percent proficient
 	
Third-grade reading:
 	
   (Girls) 57 percent proficient
	What ways are schools doing well in the area of making connections and reading for meaning?
	
	What factors are contributing to success for schools that do not receive support (Turnaround/OFIP)?
	
	Literacy block components are implemented inconsistently.
	
	Support to OFIP schools had little impact on making connections on EQAO reports (due to late start, three months of support).
	
	Does writing production (frequency/volume) influence reading connections?
	
	Is our monitoring process routine and frequent enough to provide feedback to schools and to professional learning teams (PLTs)?
		All teachers and principals will be in-serviced in the elementary reading assessment framework and guide.
		
		Assessment *of* and *for* learning will be a focus at all schools to fully implement the elementary reading assessment framework and guide.
		
		Literacy rooms will be created at each school.
		
		There will be consistent access to, and communication of lessons from, Ontario Statistical Neighbors.
		
		The frequent use of data walls in all schools will deepen.
		
		Need system to gather and data will be analyzed for successful practices in 2008–2009.

Areas of Concern	Factors to Consider	Mitigating Strategies
(Boys) 43 percent proficient Third-grade writing: (Girls) 59 percent proficient (Boys) 40 percent proficient The degree to which data walls, shared reading, and literacy blocks are used effectively is unknown. Need evidence of all listed successful practices in 2008–2009 for data.	How were consolidation days used? What specific Turnaround School supports have been most effective over the past three years?	

Adapted from *Hastings and Prince Edward District School Board, 2007, used with permission*

Superintendent Sue Zook in Hawthorn devoted an entire academic year to developing internal expertise in terms of school improvement design, implementation, and evaluation, and to stretching her very capable leadership team by creating a template that captures data in novel ways. Hawthorn asked for information documenting acts of leadership such as communication strategies and acts of teaching such as collaboration. By gathering information about how leaders communicate and how teachers collaborate, Hawthorn had information at its fingertips about the degree to which best practices were present in the day-to-day operation of each school. Karen Olker, coordinator of professional development, notes,

> We discovered that school improvement was much more complex than we anticipated, and we assumed high levels of implementation that just was not occurring as consistently as we'd hoped. We also discovered that schools attempt to accomplish too much, and have learned to go slow to go fast. We use the improvement process to reveal the complexity of the goals we aspire to. (personal communication, June 12, 2009)

A comprehensive needs assessment often reveals how quickly leaders assume deep implementation rather than deliberately gather data to verify that implementation with any precision. For example, Hastings and Prince Edward identified a wide range of successful practices and, in the process, discovered that the degree to which balanced literacy components were present was not clear. Their template helped them discover a need for greater precision in data, and one of their major concerns was to provide that evidence in subsequent plans.

This first step in the planning cycle will determine the range of possibilities from which the school will choose to improve current practice. Schools that systematically gather data about teaching and leading—particularly by examining the degree to which common strategies are delivered, collaboration is practiced, and accountability structures are repeated—will have a much broader and deeper understanding of the factors that impact student achievement.

We will now examine the next step in the planning phase—inquiry. While governing agencies often encourage this process, it remains the most elusive and overlooked of school improvement essentials.

Inquiry Process

DECEMBER 8, 10:30 A.M. As Byron drove to the diner after the morning planning session with Helen and the rest of the team, he realized the now monthly meetings with his former student, Dr. Olsen, were beginning to approximate a coaching relationship—with the student coaching the principal. Even more surprisingly, Byron looked forward to these meetings. He arrived early and ordered for both men. Yohannon walked in, looked around the room, then waved as he found Byron's table. "Sorry I'm late, Byron. Bring me up to speed."

"Well, I did go back and identify the number of initiatives we had on the table," Byron said. "Henry used SurveyMonkey to gather the data from the staff and found at least fourteen curriculum issues underway that are outside of our school improvement plan. We can deal with that, but what shocked me was the fact that even though I limited this year's improvement plan to three goals, that translates into three core strategies applied across eight departments for a minimum of twenty-four different approaches! I'm not sure what to scale back."

Yohannon paused before responding. "OK, do these data include scheduled school events such as the science fair or art show?"

"Of course not, we plan to be fragmented," Byron joked, shaking his head. Both men sat pensively while the waitress refilled coffees.

"That complexity sounds pretty overwhelming, Byron. When we pursued two major projects for eighteen months with all the resources you would ever want and three pharmaceutical labs at our beck and call, we were taxed to meet deadlines and found ourselves trying to do too much too quickly. I learned the importance of narrowing the scope of our work. During the past year, did anyone question the need for three goals or point out how the details of execution were frustrating the effort?"

"No one. In years past, most of our plans had even more goals."

"How often did you actually complete the action steps in your plans?"

Byron shook his head. "Sometimes we reached our goals in terms of student achievement, but I don't know for sure. Not often enough."

Nodding, the scientist added, "All right, we've identified the problem. Ideas for your next step?"

Narrowing the Focus

Inquiry is the process of narrowing the focus by examining data in such a way as to reveal the critical areas that need to be addressed. The process includes triangulating the comprehensive forms of data; identifying correlations that reveal the strongest practices; forming questions that remain unanswered; and juxtaposing that information to generate a few, prioritized hypotheses. We found inquiry to be a factor that also contributes to greater gains for schools when the process is intentional rather than incidental or absent in the improvement sequence. Figure 3.2 describes the experience for another large school system, Houston Independent School District (HISD) in Texas. The Texas Assessment of Knowledge and Skills (TAKS™) is one of the longest standing statewide assessments in the United States. It represents Texas' primary measure of student performance to designate school status for AYP and for community recognition or sanction.

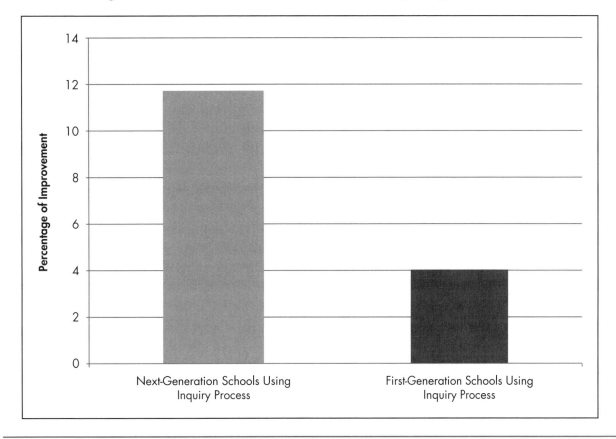

Figure 3.2: Houston ISD science gains on TAKS as a result of inquiry, 2006–2007.
Leadership and Learning Center, 2007b, used with permission

In this case, schools with a clearly defined inquiry process in their improvement plan experienced almost three times the gains of schools without a process of inquiry.

Reflection is a key attribute of inquiry, and next-generation leaders will be those who approach school improvement systematically, devote time to reflect, to think, and then to act. Teachers prepared for the next generation work interdependently on improvement teams.

The inquiry process should identify correlations between teaching and leading practices and gains in student achievement. By discerning these factors from the data, teams will be able to narrow the focus and prioritize planned actions with the greatest promise of success. To accomplish this, we recommend a process of triangulation, through which student achievement results are examined in terms of their relationship, or lack thereof, with antecedent practices such as those discussed in the comprehensive needs-assessment section.

Triangulation

Triangulation is solving for an unknown on the basis of known information. For example, suppose that as teachers, we know IEP students performed below their peers in mathematics problem solving. We also know that they made larger percentage gains in the proportion of students who passed the state assessment. Upon further investigation, we learn that the coteachers who served the IEP students implemented a new strategy in their inclusion classroom. Let's assume our inquiry found the following: (1) the teachers modeled explanation of reasoning as they introduced new concepts and reviewed familiar concepts daily; (2) students verbally explained their reasoning when called upon, and all in-class and homework assignments required an explanation of reasoning in writing; and (3) IEP students were held to the same expectation, but were allowed to use some sentence-stem prompts for the first grading period, after which the stems were removed. The outcome of this single change resulted in twice the gain for IEP students than their general education peers, and four times the gain when compared to IEP students in the same grade at other middle schools.

Triangulation examines the interactions between these practices and student achievement patterns to isolate the unknown, and our example offers a number of clues: (1) the only change was in terms of the selected instructional strategy; (2) the method required students to think about their own mental models; (3) the teachers, by modeling their own thinking to explain their reasoning, helped students understand how to process new material; and (4) because students were required to write, they had to thoroughly understand the math challenges they were facing and opportunities to guess or check out from the lesson were minimized. After generating statements about how the data revealed that the explaining reasoning protocol was a contributing factor to the achievement gain, and developing questions that warranted additional data (Why did we see the gap close so quickly?), teams can confidently generate a hypothesis for action. In this case, the hypothesis the team generates might read something like this:

> IF all co-teaching classrooms at our school implement the explaining reasoning protocol at least three days each week,
>
> THEN students will be better prepared to achieve proficiency on the state examination in mathematics problem solving.

Triangulation, by examining student achievement in terms of adult actions like those described here, should yield a few hypotheses of action that then guide the development of SMART goals and precise action steps to achieve them (action steps are derived from the IF statements, and goals are derived from the THEN statements).

Pareto's Law

Another tool of inquiry to rule out extraneous data as part of the comprehensive needs assessment is the use of Pareto's Law, or the 80/20 principle. Economists often talk about Pareto's Law, which is the idea that in any set of data, a few (20 percent) are vital and many (80 percent) are trivial. Vilfredo Pareto, a twentieth-century Italian economist, observed that 20 percent of the people owned 80 percent of the wealth. After Pareto made his observation and created his formula, many others observed similar phenomena in their own areas of expertise (Koch, 1998). Pareto's Law is now used liberally to describe almost anything. For example, 80 percent of the U.S. healthcare budget is attributed to 20 percent of the variables most directly related to poor health. Eighty percent of the beer consumed in the United States is estimated to be consumed by roughly 20 percent of the population.

The value of Pareto's Law to school improvement for the next generation is its ability to help us identify the 20 percent of information that matters most. Successful inquiry efforts always rule out inconclusive and extraneous data while ruling in patterns and trends that spotlight the most meaningful and useful data. Pareto's Law is applied to reading in figure 3.3.

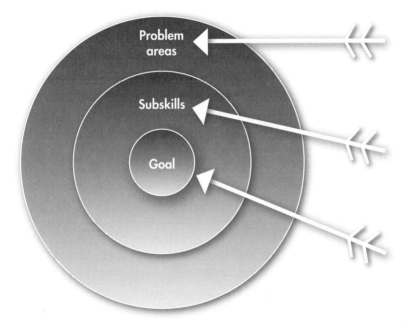

Identify which areas of applied reading—**reading**, writing, or mathematics—are most problematic for our students.

Identify which subskills— vocabulary, decoding, or **comprehension**—are most problematic for our students.

Identify the goal as helping students find the main idea and **draw conclusions** from words in context, supporting facts, and details.

Figure 3.3: Targeting instructional improvement efforts.

School improvement teams or collaborative PLC/data teams of teachers will leverage an effective process of inquiry by applying Pareto's Law to drill deeper to identify the most likely place to begin an improvement effort. Both PLCs and data teams are defined teacher teams that adhere to an established agenda to examine student work, create common assessments, and implement common solutions to address needs identified in student work samples.

If improvement plans include a proficient inquiry process, educators will have narrowed the focus sufficiently to generate one or more hypotheses that inform possible goal statements and action steps or implementation strategies. Consider how the hypothesis in figure 3.4 serves as a launching pad for a SMART goal and possible focused action steps or strategies.

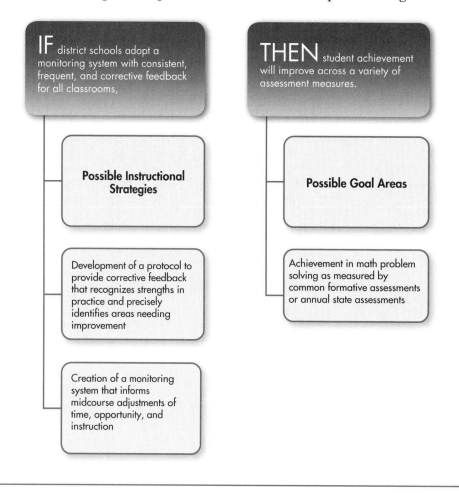

Figure 3.4: Hypothesis as a critical function of the inquiry process.

This hypothesis illustrates how effective planning helps schools increase the level of precision applied when designing school improvement changes. The inquiry process is short-circuited when school improvement teams hastily jump to popular current practices or favorite programs as solutions to identified needs. If, however, teams take time to reflect on causal factors and clearly define priorities, improvement plans become aligned, focused, precise documents that produce both SMART goals and informed, powerful strategies for action.

John Taylor, principal of the Ben Davis Ninth Grade Center in the Metropolitan School District (MSD) of Wayne Township in Indianapolis, finds this process particularly useful. His team examined their data and found that both struggling and high-achieving students had fewer office referrals, better attendance, better grades, and even higher reading comprehension scores when they enrolled in biology than in other courses throughout the school. After triangulating the professional practices data available by content and grade level, John and his team discovered a set of strategies that were key to the gains realized, and named them the "biology protocol" (personal communication, January 18, 2009). They then generated the following hypothesis:

> IF we replicate aspects of the collaborative protocol used by biology across content areas,
>
> THEN student achievement in reading comprehension will improve both schoolwide and for IEP students.

The result was more than a great set of strategies for all content areas (such as Japanese lesson study or careful item analysis of each common formative assessment by department), but also a process that would guide their entire school improvement plan and reduce the number of goals from four to one. John and his team discovered that by conducting a thorough process of inquiry, they were much better able to identify precisely what needs to be done to improve student achievement. The strategy may not work, but without this process, it is likely that John's school would have continued to pursue separate improvement goals for reading, math, writing, and perhaps science. Instead, he discovered a way to make the most successful best practice at his school a common one, and saved time and effort in the process.

The inquiry process is part science (use of triangulation or Pareto's Law and reliance on needs assessment evidence), but it is also an art, in which informed teams apply their collective wisdom to examine all the possible paths they might take and select the most promising path to improve achievement. The process of generating hypotheses to focus efforts sets the stage for quality SMART goals and insightful action plans.

SMART Goals

DECEMBER 16, 2:30 P.M. Mi Lai brought the improvement plan to the English/language arts department meeting and placed a flip-chart tent that stated the school goal for their department on the conference table:

> Goal 1: Students at KCHS will show increased achievement in reading on the spring 2012 High School Performance Assessment (HSPA). Specific improvement will be made by the IEP subgroup in all reading areas and performance strands (such as comprehension, literary analysis, and vocabulary).

"The school improvement process team adopted our idea about higher-order thinking skills, but challenged everyone to focus on closing the gap for IEP students. Before responding, I want to say that Helen and I were skeptical at first, but Byron and the entire team made a strong case for targeting the group of students who struggle with a skill. The team discussed how focusing on this subgroup will help every teacher in every department emphasize key language arts skills that engage every student. It was really pretty exciting, because for each IEP student who meets proficiency on the HSPA, three other proficient students achieve advanced. I don't know how that works, but there's been a correlation for the past two years. It seemed perfectly appropriate to continue to raise the bar for all students while using the group least likely to succeed as our measure of success. Joanne, the language arts coordinator from the district, says this phenomenon is really pretty common. What do you think?"

Henry spoke first. "I think it's fine, as long as they don't flood my class with special education kids like they did two years ago."

Mary was concerned on several fronts. "Mi Lai, I know everyone wants us all to become special education teachers by some edict, but I don't know what they need, I didn't go to school to teach those students, and I resent it." The team began to talk among themselves, until Mi Lai brought them back.

"Thanks for getting the elephant on the table, Mary, but the plan doesn't reassign you or even presume that you provide special education, only that each of us monitors our progress to make sure we ask for help and get the support we need when we need it. It means . . ."

"Excuse me, Mi Lai," Scott interrupted, "but I think I have some information that will help us get on the same page. Mary, wasn't Michael Forest in your English lit class?"

"Yes, why?"

"He is on an IEP. Henry, did you know Elisa Ortez was also an IEP student? Both students earned Bs or better in your classes. What Mi Lai is talking about is merely making our goal about all kids, not lowering our standards or watering down our curriculum. I like the fact that we are making higher-order thinking our strategy, and IEP kids need to be challenged in this way too."

"Thanks for pointing that out, Scott," Mi Lai said. "I was unaware as well, but I do know that if we don't help IEP kids achieve at the same high levels other kids do, our school is in trouble. Byron made it very clear that ignoring this achievement gap will put us in need of improvement, and then the state will tell us what to do." More grumbling and talking with neighbors ensued.

Oscar stood to get everyone's attention. "I have a different question. If all this works out, how will we know if we met our goal or not?" All eyes turned back to the goal statement on the flip-chart tent.

Oscar's question about goal setting is critical: unless goals are explicit enough to be measured as having been met or not, the goal is neither instructive nor useful. Hence the third step of effective planning is developing SMART (specific, measurable, achievable, relevant, timely) goals—a familiar acronym in educational circles, as well as in the private and public sectors. Goals for the next generation of schools need to be smart not only in terms of the acronym's criteria, but also in terms of informing stakeholders of the distance that needs to be closed and the group of students for whom success will indicate that the entire school is on track. Because goals describe a preferred future—that is, a vision—it is critical that the content of the SMART goal–setting process be informed by both evidence and professional judgment.

SMART Goals Are Specific

Specificity is essential to create an effective goal statement. Is a goal to "improve reading" specific? Does *specific* mean specific content area or specific student group? SMART goals always utilize explicit criteria to minimize interpretation and establish a common understanding of terms. "Improve reading" tells us the general goal, but "improve reading comprehension" provides a greater level of clarity and understanding. "Improve skills in drawing inferences from text or making connections between the text and one's life experience" is even more instructive about the area of need.

To classroom teachers, the goal to improve reading communicates a message that working on reading is the focus: "Since I work on reading every day, I will do my best to continue to provide reading instruction to the best of my ability." When the specificity increases to reading comprehension, the message is to emphasize reading comprehension and augment it with other elements of reading (vocabulary, phonemic awareness, word choice, decoding, and so on). The increased specificity also increases the level of focus and clarifies expectations.

Specificity needs to extend to students as well. The conventional wisdom in school improvement is that goals should be for everyone and that targeting specific learning needs essentially ignores other students. If gaps in math problem-solving achievement exist only for students receiving free and reduced lunch, should the school ignore those data simply because goals are supposed to be written for the entire school? In such a scenario, writing a generic improvement goal for the entire school (math scores will increase 2 percent from 84 percent proficient to 86 percent proficient) misses the point that some students need an intervention more than others. Goals should follow needs, not traditions, and schools need to become comfortable with writing goals for groups of students rather than the entire school population. By addressing skill deficits experienced by a specific targeted group, improved instruction for that area will not only address a schoolwide area of need, but will also refine and enhance instruction for all. Will students who are already at standard on math problem solving be less so because the improvement plan establishes a problem-solving goal to close the achievement gap? The following sample SMART goal illustrates how it is possible to set a goal that addresses the achievement gaps for targeted students at both ends of the continuum.

> By June 1, 20____, students will independently make connections between information and ideas in nonfiction content areas and their personal experience as measured by improvement from 57 percent of students at level 3 and 4 on the provincial reading comprehension assessment for all grades to 74 percent at level 3 and 4 and a decrease in the percentage of level 1 and 2 students from 50 percent to 22 percent.

Many states and Canadian provinces have annual high-stakes assessments that differentiate student performance in terms of a four- or five-point scale. In our example, those students scoring at the lowest levels (1 and 2) were targeted for gains, while students at the proficient level (3 and 4) were also targeted for improvement. Schools and districts that substitute identified groups by ethnicity, gender, family income, or language can achieve the same level of clarity and focus. SMART goals also describe the assessment to be used as a measure of effectiveness and goal attainment.

Consider again the KCHS goal: "Students at KCHS will show increased achievement in reading on the spring 2012 High School Performance Assessment (HSPA). Specific improvement will be made by the IEP subgroup in all reading areas and performance strands (such as comprehension, literary analysis, and vocabulary)." The goal does address the need for the subgroup (IEP students) to improve reading across all strand areas, but it fails to target the strand in which improvement is most needed or most valuable in terms of building proficiency in reading. Goals that state that everything needs to improve do not narrow the focus; goals that specify the need at the strand level communicate without ambiguity the target for improvement.

SMART Goals Are Measurable

SMART goals are made quantifiable by simply indicating the baseline level on a selected measure and then pinpointing the desired change in performance. Some suggest goals should be general statements that provide enough latitude to allow educators to explain how goals are being met without being held to a fixed target. This runs counter to an axiom of a standards-based education: standards (targets and expectations) remain fixed, while time and opportunity to achieve them vary. Creating generic goal statements that provide latitude to "spin" results is also dissonant with the concept of transparency in communication. Measurable goals, whether for states, provinces, districts, schools, classrooms, students, and even nations, should say what they mean in unambiguous terms.

SMART Goals Are Achievable

Goals that are achievable for the next generation are not calculated to simply repeat "realistic" gains from previous years. Instead, goals are viewed through the lens of academic health, and must literally be achievable for the next generation of learners. If the goal is not sufficiently targeted to close achievement gaps within three to five years, then it is less about achievement and more about maintaining the status quo. An achievable SMART goal will also narrow the achievement gaps by differentiating targets by student subgroup. Figure 3.5 illustrates actual assessment gains in Ontario as a result of creating achievable goal statements.

The achievement gains for Ontario schools on the Educational Quality and Accountability Office (EQAO) exams reveal that goals designed to close achievement gaps are themselves a predictor of student achievement. The schools above represented almost one hundred thousand students and the data, while not definitive, suggests that achievable goals in terms of closing achievement gaps represent a best practice in leadership that serves as an antecedent for improved student achievement.

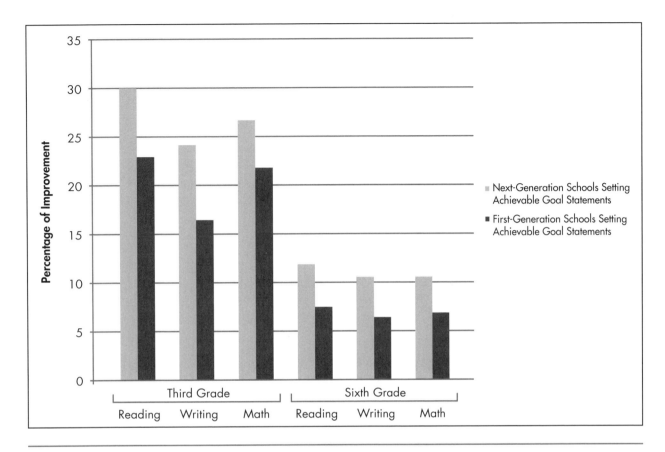

Figure 3.5: Ontario cumulative gains on the EQAO as a result of achievable goals designed to close the achievement gap, 2002–2007.

Leadership and Learning Center, 2008, used with permission

In our KCHS case study, it is reasonable to infer that the team hoped to close the achievement gap because they targeted the lower-performing group of students, but their goal statement is vague because it does not specify what they need to know, what is expected, or what needs to occur for the goal to be achieved.

SMART Goals Are Relevant

Relevant goals target the most urgent areas of need that emerge from the comprehensive needs assessment, rather than reinforce use of a popular program or familiar content. The evidence discussed and revealed in the comprehensive needs assessment informs relevant goals. Denise Wiedemann, coordinator of research and accountability for Clark County, Nevada, puts it this way: "If we help students create a beautiful map of Texas, it won't do them much good if they are trying to get from Reno to Las Vegas" (personal communication, February 11, 2009). Denise understands the need for the SMART goal to have a clear relationship to other school improvement phases. By following the evidence, school improvement teams deliberately pursue changes in practice to translate best practice into common practice. KCHS, in this case, did select their targeted group of students (IEP) as a function of the large achievement gap depicted in table 1.1 (page 7). The comprehensive needs analysis and the process of inquiry inform their goal statement, and, therefore, their goal is SMART in terms of relevancy.

SMART Goals Are Timely

Timely goals describe a specific, limited amount of time in which to accomplish specific, measurable, achievable, and relevant SMART goals. The adage that what gets measured gets done is more aptly represented as what gets scheduled gets done. Our KCHS scenario illustrates how it is all too possible for schools adhering to current school improvement practices to meet the standard in some aspects, fall short in others, and come away empty without a goal statement that is instructive at all to faculty members. For instance, their goal—"Students at KCHS will show increased achievement in reading on the spring 2012 High School Performance Assessment (HSPA). Specific improvement will be made by the IEP subgroup in all reading areas and performance strands (such as comprehension, literary analysis, and vocabulary)"—fails to include an instructive timeline.

Final Thoughts

When you think about the planning phase of the improvement process, imagine the work and its flow as a funnel (fig. 3.6). Each step connects to the next in the cycle of continuous improvement. First, comprehensive needs assessment provides a three-dimensional view of teaching and learning, broadly exploring successes and challenges. Next, inquiry sifts through the data, identifies cause-and-effect relationships, and generates hypotheses for action. Finally, those hypotheses provide the genesis for SMART goals.

Quality planning is a collaborative, reflective process that builds a foundation for continuous improvement. To respond to the next generation of school improvement demands and opportunities, each step of this phase is critical—none are optional. Chapter 4 describes the next phase of the school improvement cycle, implementation, in which ambitious goals are translated into demonstrable results.

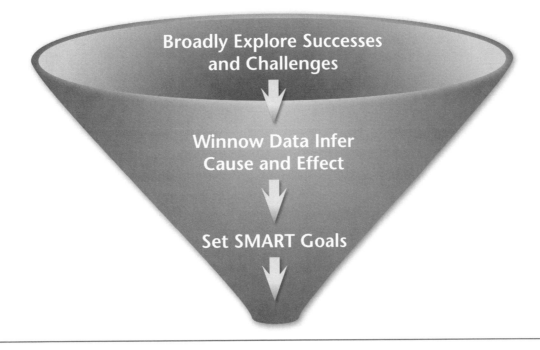

Figure 3.6: The planning phase of school improvement.

Key Questions for Team Study

A needs assessment is only comprehensive when evidence describes learning, teaching, and leading.

What is the premise behind this statement? How does it apply to the improvement plans generated by your school or district?

Inquiry generates hypotheses for improvement.

Why is this necessary as a prerequisite step to developing SMART goals?

What needs to be done to minimize the tendency to jump to solutions in school improvement planning?

SMART goals are only smart when they protect the focus for improvement.

What is the premise behind this statement? To what degree do you agree and why?

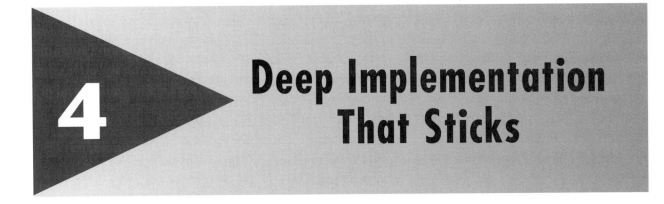

Deep Implementation That Sticks

Always sweat the small stuff.

—Rudy Giuliani

DECEMBER 22, 10:00 A.M. The diner was busy with a midmorning rush. Because of the holiday break, Byron enjoyed a meeting without the traditional coat and tie. He handed Yohannon the school improvement team's latest work as he slid into the booth.

"Thanks for bringing part of your school improvement plan for me to peruse," Yohannon said.

"No problem," Byron responded, as he lifted his coffee cup.

"These planning templates look different than the flow charts and project management charts that I typically see, so I have a few questions."

Byron smiled. "Why am I not surprised?"

Yohannon paused as he scrutinized the documents. "I'm curious. Are you tracking the changes you planned, or are you tracking student achievement as an indicator of those changes?"

Byron scanned his copy.

Yohannon pointed at one item. "The plan calls for teachers to implement HSPA warm-up drills and for teachers to use advanced placement texts and syllabi to increase rigor, right?"

Byron looked at the item and nodded. "Right."

Yohannon continued, "Help me, but I think the plan also calls for teachers to incorporate the reading initiatives about higher-order thinking into their lesson plans. Am I reading it correctly?"

"Absolutely, and we repeat that expectation in terms of math skills and wellness issues. We require our entire faculty to use these action steps to guide how they make a few basic changes to their classroom practice." Byron was anxious to defend the hard work of his improvement team.

"The action steps make perfect sense. It's just that the measures of progress are all student tests, with one exception—lesson plans about the reading initiative. Even that action step describes how teams meet together in departments rather than saying anything about how higher-order thinking becomes a reality in the lesson plans. Aren't you most interested in tracking practices that will yield improved achievement? If your lesson plans monitored how often teachers used higher-order thinking, you would know that students were being challenged, right?"

"With all due respect, Yohannon, our teachers are professionals who apply their craft in unique ways. They won't be using the same lessons. We have eight large and diverse departments who will be implementing very different content and lesson plans. Our departments will discuss the degree to which the action step will be implemented, and they are already doing that monthly."

"All right." Yohannon leaned back in his chair. "Give me one example of what one department will do and how you will know it is being done well and not just in a mediocre fashion."

During the silence that followed, both men knew for the first time that their cordial relationship was strained. It had been fun up until now. Byron frowned, then smiled. "These meetings with you are valuable, Yohannon. I guess I just didn't expect to be moved out of my comfort zone every single month!"

"OK, Byron, I've said many times that I don't know your business, but I do know a little about breaking through when solutions are not obvious. Your team knows their craft, but I'm trying to understand what is intended in your plan for improvement. When the action step speaks about teaching, and your measures speak about student learning, and there is no means to determine how well the action step was implemented, or how consistently, or how frequently, it just looks like it might confuse some and send mixed messages to others, that's all."

"I know my faculty. I think I can assume that teams will work out the details."

The physicist lowered his voice and inquired, "And how is that working for you in terms of achieving your goals for kids?"

Former New York City mayor Rudy Giuliani describes his leadership strategy to "always sweat the small stuff" as the most important factor in reducing rampant levels of both petty and serious crime that once characterized the streets and subways of New York (Giuliani, 2002, p. 47). Giuliani made it a point to meet weekly with key department leaders, and in those meetings he received very specific reports about granular improvements such as reduction of turnstile jumping, jaywalking crimes, graffiti reduction, the number of broken windows in blight neighborhoods, and the number of employee complaints. These and many other apparently "small" challenges were monitored and measured as a way of preventing small issues from becoming major crises. For school improvement efforts to be implemented deeply and to succeed, the same attention to the mundane is required.

Chapter 2 outlined a framework to identify best practices that need to become common practices, but the most effective planning process only ensures an optimum *opportunity* for success. Real improvement is contingent on the degree to which teachers and leaders implement the knowledge they have about what works and what doesn't work. *The Knowing-Doing Gap* (Pfeffer & Sutton, 2000) makes a compelling case that most organizations avoid acting on what they know, assuming instead that the attractiveness of the proposed change to a few will translate, unassisted, into enthusiastic support from all. In their sequel, *Hard Facts, Dangerous Half-Truths, and Total Nonsense*, Pfeffer and Sutton (2006) explain how confidence in the power of selected innovations often overshadows the need for precise, granular implementation. The result was that many improvement efforts are focused on the right thing to do, but end up being executed in the wrong way.

This chapter focuses on how things get done by describing five best practices for effective implementation. These practices define master plan design, targeted research-based strategies, professional development focus, professional development implementation, and parental engagement. Each describes opportunities to sweat the small stuff and advance the changes most important to the success of improvement efforts. First, however, we describe four common pitfalls of implementation to be aware of.

Four Pitfalls of Implementation

In this section, we explore why "sweating the small stuff" is so important to establishing deep levels of implementation and to sustaining those levels. School improvement efforts often fall victim to the following problems: blaming the kids, blaming the program, casual selection of strategies, and fragmentation.

Blaming the Kids

As educators, we tend to be rather self-effacing. When students do well, we attribute their success to the cohort being a great class, or we give undue credit to the program or model of instruction or curriculum design. When students do poorly, we attribute their lack of success to the cohort being a difficult class of students, or we ascribe blame to the program, instructional model, or curriculum. More often, parents are targeted as the source of student learning problems, but whether we blame students or parents, the exercise rarely helps us design curriculum or deliver instruction.

Rather than being modest about our achievements, we should take credit for successful efforts and understand with some clarity that what we actually did made a difference for children. We must replace the mindset that attributes every change in student performance to luck and/or the students alone. In reality, successful student learning is largely the result of quality teaching deeply implemented with fidelity (Wenglinsky, 2002). Lack of success is more often than not the result of inconsistent instruction when some apply a best practice with fidelity, and others do not. Students are certainly responsible for their achievement, but teaching determines the degree to which they understand content; demonstrate proficient skills at applying that understanding; and retain, synthesize, or evaluate their own learning. Teaching matters. Schmoker (2006) under-scores this point in his book *Results Now: How We Can Achieve Unprecedented Improvements in Teaching and Learning*, when he states, "A focus on learning, on assessment results, becomes the leverage for improvements in teaching, which is only as good as its impact on learning" (p. 126). Schmoker's challenge to educators parallels Yohannon's challenge to Byron regarding the omission in the KCHS improvement plan: the plans must monitor and measure not only how well students perform, but the degree to which the adult practices employed by teachers and leadership impact student performance.

Blaming the Program

Unfortunately, schools that experience less-than-stellar school improvement outcomes often choose to blame the innovation rather than the degree to which the innovation was executed with fidelity. When the next innovation falls short of initial expectations, the cycle continues—the problem must surely have been the program or model adopted.

Schools are organized in a loosely coupled fashion (Elmore, 2000; Weick, 1976) in which teachers are allowed considerable latitude in determining not only what content is taught, but also how it's taught. Administrators are also afforded considerable autonomy, as evident in terms of supervision of principals; specifically, Reeves (2009a), in his book *Assessing Educational Leaders*, notes that far too many school districts utilize leadership evaluation instruments that contain ambiguous standards and include performance expectations that are unclear. Thus, leadership supervision policies and instruments are often loosely coupled with the day-to-day actions of leaders. Elmore (2000) describes one insidious aspect of loosely coupled systems worth noting: a presumption of inviolability in teaching and leadership that is both cultural and unspoken. If results are not as we hoped or planned, the explanation is all too often that elements of the program were flawed. Understanding the relationship between our actions and student achievement is the heart of being a professional educator, and school improvement is the vehicle that causes our collective ability to make a difference most obvious. Isn't it interesting how we attribute success to programs, even though no program engages students, no program ever modified instruction, and no program is capable of responding to the simultaneous needs of diverse students during a fifty-minute high school period, or one hundred minutes of literacy block for elementary students? Programs matter, but not as much as teaching.

Casual Selection of Strategies

Virtually every profession or industry during the late twentieth century embraced the notion of "benchmarking" or learning from the experience of others. Schools and school districts frequently engage in "opportunistic surveillance" (Rogers, 1995, p. 393), in which they search for new ideas and adopt best practices they have observed elsewhere or read about in research. When the most visible attribute of a best practice—rather than the most important—is adopted, however, school improvement efforts suffer due to casual selection. For example, professional learning communities (PLCs) are widely recognized and accepted as predictors of improved student achievement, and thousands of PLCs are in place around the world today. Some refer to themselves as learning teams, others as data teams (Ainsworth & Viegut, 2006), others still as whole-faculty study groups (Murphy & Lick, 2001). The most visible aspect of all is the formation of teacher teams who meet during the school day. However, the formation of a team in itself is unlikely to predict success unless the critical attributes of PLCs are collectively established, routinely monitored, measured, and adjusted according to the team's reflection, evidence, candor, and synergy.

Professional learning communities, by definition, invite teams of teachers to become the masters of their own craft in terms of how they present curriculum, design assessments, evaluate results, and deliver instruction. Teachers become experts by developing skills and knowledge that equip them to answer the following questions (DuFour et al., 2005):

▶ What is it we want all students to learn?

▶ How will we know when each student has mastered the essential learning?

▶ How will we respond when a student experiences initial difficulty in learning?

▶ How will we deepen the learning for students who have already mastered essential knowledge and skills? (p. 15)

School improvement strategies need to be sufficiently explicit and granular to address the critical, most important aspects of professional learning communities—in this case, the ability to respond with confidence to these four questions. Creating time to meet is very different from building a functioning data team (Reeves, 2009a) or professional learning community (DuFour et al., 2005) in which members collectively examine student work and determine which instructional strategies will improve achievement.

Casual selection of strategies may produce some benefit, but it seldom produces as much benefit as more precise, explicit, and defined strategies. A second example of how educators sometimes casually choose the most visible strategy illustrates the problem in more depth. The organization of research-based instructional strategies into nine categories through a comprehensive meta-analysis (Marzano et al., 2001) represents a huge breakthrough in terms of applying lessons from the research to the classroom. When school improvement teams respond casually by inviting each classroom teacher to identify the category of strategy in a lesson rather than determining which strategy is best suited to the content or levels of readiness of the students, teams miss an opportunity for real improvement. The nine broad strategies describe very familiar practices, such as similarities and differences, and a casual process may accept worksheets with matching items as evidence of instruction in similarities and differences. However, when that strategy is selected strategically, the same classroom could deliver instruction about similes, metaphors, and analogies that engage students in meaningful higher-level thinking and writing.

Casual selection opens the door for performance that is dated, predictable, and mediocre. Sweating the small stuff in terms of implementing school improvement strategies increases the likelihood that best practices will become common practice.

Fragmentation

A final pitfall that leads to low levels of implementation is the tendency to compartmentalize the work of school improvement into familiar categories. For example, first-generation school improvement plans frequently worked within a paradigm that required two or three academic goals and one affective goal each year. Schools throughout the 1980s, 1990s, and the first decade of the twenty-first century insisted on separate goals for reading/language arts, mathematics, and writing, and some added a fourth academic goal for science as well, particularly when science became a fixture within the state high-stakes assessment programs. This fragmentation makes it difficult for teams to identify those small, well-focused actions that leverage the prospect of producing significant, enduring improvements—and it minimizes the opportunity to make connections across disciplines. Fragmentation encourages departments or grade levels to continue to function as silos of learning in which isolation and autonomy trump focus and improvement.

Fragmentation introduces complexity that becomes a barrier to focused improvement efforts. Schools like our hypothetical Kelly County High School already have multiple events occurring every day before they consider adding a single school improvement initiative, and their experience reveals the effort and coordination needed to achieve any goals. Hence, SMART goals, as the launching pad of planning, influence the capacity we have to successfully implement the goals with fidelity. Fewer goals are one way to reduce complexity and ensure a common focus on improvement efforts because they communicate the least number of targets for students, staff, and parents to identify.

There is both a practical and empirical rationale supporting this axiom. Many times, goals are not held in common by the school, and they require consistent implementation. If teachers can opt in or out of specific goals, school improvement becomes a misnomer as changes in practice become optional. Plans to improve practice require professional learning to enable faculty to master the new strategy or protocol. The slightest improvement in practice requires some modification of current practice to make room for the improvement. Figure 4.1 describes the relationship between gains and the number of school improvement goals in Clark County School District, Las Vegas, Nevada.

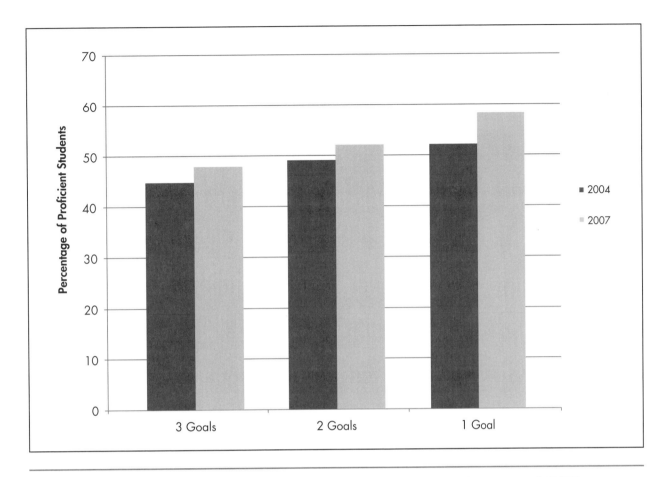

Figure 4.1: Clark County School District achievement gains on the CRT and HSPE as a result of the number of goals, 2004–2007.

Reeves et al., 2007, used with permission

The notion of fewer goals creating more focus and better results is equally evident in business. When Steve Jobs rejoined Apple as CEO in 1997, no fewer than fifteen products were sold, but by 1998, four products had replaced all fifteen, and market share skyrocketed (Pfeffer & Sutton, 2006). The same was true a decade later for automobiles—Honda produced ten vehicles, while Chrysler produced thirty but sold far fewer overall (Index of the Web, n.d.). Chapter 8 elaborates on the concept of simplicity to address the complex issues of teaching and learning, and the even more complex task of guiding change and improving practice.

Sweating the small stuff is a process of leveraging the mundane day-to-day operational tasks to relentlessly pursue school improvement goals. Pfeffer and Sutton (2006) suggest that sticking with proven practices may be boring, asking rhetorically, "Isn't bland old excellence a better fate than an exciting new failure?" (p. 43). We need to learn from the events around us every bit as much as we learn from the latest external innovation. Figure 4.2 (page 70) depicts ten acts of leadership through which leaders earn credibility every day through excellent decisions or foolish mistakes evident to all. Leaders create opportunities, ensure best practices become common practice by replicating them schoolwide, and work every day to help their staff generate hypotheses in their work. The most effective leaders provide feedback that challenges staff to make improvements. Strong leaders also develop their own expertise in data analysis, research, and communication. Leaders demonstrate skills and credibility in the mundane aspects of schools and they create the connections—and balance—needed for deep and sustainable implementation that improves schools.

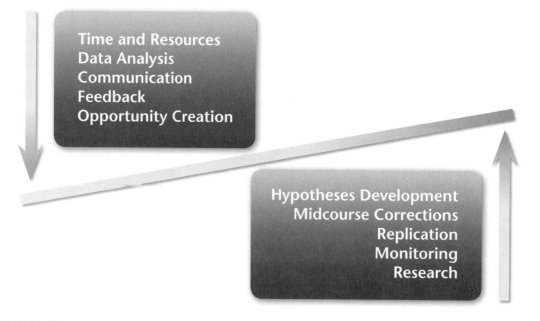

Figure 4.2: Acts of leadership.
Adapted from *White, 2005a*

A real estate adage describes the basis for property value in three words: *location, location, location.* For school improvement, deep implementation can also be summed up in three words: *connections, connections, connections.* How those connections are communicated, established, deepened, and sustained distinguishes successful improvement efforts from unsuccessful. Effective improvement efforts address these acts of leadership systematically in their master plan design, as we will explore in the next section. Leaders who carefully manage these acts of leadership to promote dialogue and inquiry will build the foundation for the next generation of school improvement through a culture of evidence.

Five Best Practices

Evidence from the field proves the importance of attention to granular, incremental, and progressive implementation and the danger of making assumptions about professional practice. We will explore five best practices of effective implementation: master plan design, targeted research-based strategies, professional development focus, professional development implementation, and parental engagement. We will give special attention to the need to plan sequential and coordinated timelines, create explicit descriptions of planned action steps, ensure fidelity of implementation, and provide opportunities for distributed leadership.

Master Plan Design

A master plan design is the umbrella framework that describes the details and coordination—the "how" rather than the "hoped for"—of targeted research-based strategies, professional development focus, professional development implementation, and parental engagement. Consider the relationship in the Houston Independent School District between the gains in student achievement that occurred with an exemplary master plan design (as determined by use of a common rubric) versus a plan that was reviewed and scored by the authors as needing improvement (fig. 4.3).

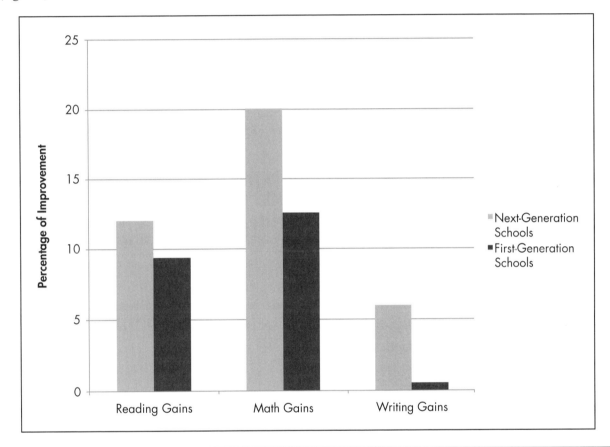

Figure 4.3: Houston ISD achievement gains on TAKS as a result of the quality of master plan design, 2005–2007.

Leadership and Learning Center, 2007b, used with permission

In reading, mathematics, and writing, schools that provided evidence of a quality master plan design experienced higher achievement gains on the TAKS assessment than schools lacking a proficient master plan design. Four characteristics define next-generation quality in master plan design: (1) alignment and articulation, (2) champions who coordinate, (3) timelines that build capacity, and (4) progressive expectations for rigor.

Alignment and Articulation

The design of a quality master plan includes action steps that are closely articulated and aligned. The best action steps are sequential, aligned, and consistent with the master plan design purpose.

Judy Stegemann, principal of Stout Field Elementary in Wayne Township, Indiana, and her team designed master plan action steps to improve reading through literary response analysis. Stout Field's plan was to carefully ensure schoolwide participation by specifying that "all teachers will participate in focused collaborative meetings that demonstrate the use of data and evaluate the effectiveness of instructional strategies" (Stout Field Elementary, 2009, p. 16). The team created a protocol to assist faculty schoolwide to apply nine critical reading strategies from their literacy framework and to use a data collection process designed to quantify, share, and review results with the entire faculty as the year progressed. The plan created structures so that best practices would be modeled, practiced, and reviewed at grade-level meetings—with minutes distributed electronically—and the most effective of those practices would be demonstrated at least monthly before peers.

Action steps should reveal the complexity of the change desired (Darling-Hammond, 1997; Evans, 2001; Wagner & Kegan, 2005). In a profession that is much more complex than the public or practitioners acknowledge, those leading the school improvement efforts must learn to respect the challenges that they hope to overcome, or continue to experience hit-or-miss outcomes for the next generation. Lisa Lantrip, assistant superintendent for curriculum and instruction in Wayne Township, described their master plan design process this way: "We wanted our plans to serve as a blueprint for future action, not a scrapbook or record of all we are currently doing. We have worked hard to make sure improvement plans only describe actual improvements that change professional practice" (personal communication, January 12, 2009).

Champions Who Coordinate

DECEMBER 22, 10:30 A.M. Byron was glad that Yohannon had agreed to review the KCHS plan during their breakfast meeting over the winter break.

"It sounds like you have really strong teacher leadership at KCHS, especially Helen, Jose, Kim, Mi Lai, and Bill. That doesn't always come with the territory of leadership, does it?" Yohannon continued to offer questions that caused Byron to reflect on current, past, and planned practice.

"No, it doesn't come with the territory, and getting the right people requires attention to the school's culture. I often define it as unspoken rules and expectations that govern how things get done."

"Interesting observation, Byron, but is there anything you can point to that allowed you to assemble such a strong team?"

After signing the credit card slip, Byron rested his chin on his hands, and said, "I'm not sure, but I did have my antennae out when I first arrived, and when I recognized their various strengths,

I invited them to help improve the school. Bill was very committed to the contract, and when issues arose that had the potential for a possible grievance, he was quick to give me a heads-up. The first year or so I resented it, but I quickly learned that Bill's proactive protection of the contract actually protected me. When he became president of the teachers' union, we had already established a relationship. Helen, even a generation ago, was well respected as the person to go to if anything important needed to happen. Parents rave about her ability to challenge students, regardless of ability level. I can't begin to estimate the hundreds of parents who take time at graduation to let me know that Helen was the reason one student graduated and the reason another student was admitted to Harvey Mudd."

"You might remember that Helen was my British lit teacher back when I was a student," Yohannon said with a smile. "Now, what are you doing now to invite others into leadership roles?"

Byron paused, leaned back, took a sip of coffee, and replied, "I can't think of a better place for leadership to develop than our school improvement team, but you knew that."

"Yes, but in terms of who you've tasked to implement your action steps, I have no idea who your leader is. For something as important as implementing the reading initiatives, the only faculty that aren't responsible are the counselors, student support staff, and you. Why isn't Helen or Mi Lai in charge of that step?"

"Yohannon, every department is responsible, and every teacher within it is expected to carry it out. That is the whole point—we want *everyone* to own this reading initiative that advances higher-order thinking," replied Byron, again wondering whether the physicist was listening.

"Of course, but who is going to make sure the action step is coordinated, communicated, and progress charted? Byron, you need to identify a champion for every key action step or set of related action steps."

A second characteristic of master plan design is the assignment of an individual or small team to make sure each action step is fully implemented and carried out as planned. As we saw in the KCHS effort, teams and team members assumed others were responsible for carrying out the improvement plan. Far too often, plans assume that the changes in practice will simply occur, or that large numbers of persons (often classroom teachers) designated as responsible for carrying out the action step will actually do so. Everyone may be involved, and all should be responsible if the goal is school- or departmentwide. In practice, however, expecting everyone to attend to the *details* of each action step lacks the clarity needed to ensure the step's completion and full implementation; when everyone is responsible, no one is really responsible. When everyone is responsible, there is a tendency to assume that someone else will tend to the details of the implementation. Well-intentioned team members may assume that the team leader or department chair would coordinate the action step, or that someone else on the team would communicate about the status of the action step.

Assigning a champion for each major action step is both practical and a savvy distribution of leadership. It ensures that the individual selected will understand that it is his or her job to proactively coordinate and communicate that action step, rather than pursue the implementation tentatively out of fear of overstepping bounds or offending others—especially their principal or department chair. Assigning a champion communicates volumes about professionalism. Identifying individuals with unique expertise and interest demonstrates an awareness that "a team of committed people can address [a] responsibility more effectively than any one individual" (Marzano, Waters, & McNulty, 2005, p. 106), and communicates a level of respect and recognition of ability that is impossible to achieve when duties appear to be assigned arbitrarily (Kouzes & Posner, 1995; Lencioni, 2007). Inviting a faculty member to champion an action step is an important demonstration of leadership that itself distributes leadership across staff and faculty. The task of the champion is to coordinate, communicate, and chart progress, not to serve as a quasi administrator or even assume a title (such as department head). For those who are so honored by recognition of their competence, there is little need.

Timelines That Build Capacity

The third characteristic of an effective master plan design is a connected, precise, sequential timeline. Timelines such as "ongoing" or "September to June" leave too much to chance, and tend to promote the "urgency addiction" (Covey, Merrill, & Merrill, 1994, p. 35) in which the important long-term work of school improvement is trumped by the urgent and immediate. The timelines are much more apt to be met and the action step implemented as designed when timelines are strategically developed to transition from important building block action steps to full implementation. Precise timelines also help teams assess the demands being placed on staff to complete the action step in the time allotted and limit their action steps to those that can be achieved within it.

Progressive Expectations for Rigor

The fourth distinction for effective master plan design is to devise action steps that progressively increase the rigor and precision as the year passes. Jan Montgomery of Hastings and Prince Edward astutely addressed this need in her districtwide plan by implementing anchor charts in each classroom at each school to help ensure that all students were successful at making text-text connections, text-self connections, and text-world connections in all reading selections, regardless of content. An early action step was to make sure anchor charts were established in every classroom in all but one of six campuses by the end of September. By late October, principals were expected to share the best examples of anchor charts in at least one faculty meeting, thus making the expectation transparent and recognizing achievement by staff members. The final step in terms of anchor charts was planned to occur by the end of November, when exemplary anchor charts would be displayed in the boardroom. Subsequent scheduled board meetings provided opportunities for school teams to showcase their anchor charts and respond to questions and answers from policymakers. The plan established a timeline to follow during the year, and the expectation for quality was advanced through a greater degree of transparency and exposure throughout the community. Even a first-year principal was factored into this final action step; her school's action steps were scheduled to be complete by late March. Figure 4.4 offers a simple illustration of how deep implementation can be scheduled with relative ease in each plan.

October 14, 2010	January 11, 2011	April 7, 2011
30 percent of classroom teachers self-report "proficient" or higher use of Inquiry Model in Science more than twice a week.	70 percent of classroom teachers self-report "proficient" or higher use of Inquiry Model in Science more than twice a week.	100 percent of classroom teachers self-report "proficient" or higher use of Inquiry Model in Science more than twice a week.

Figure 4.4: Progressive expectations for deep implementation.

Scheduling full implementation with fidelity over time increases the likelihood that the goal will be reached. It is important to recognize that self-reporting is never as reliable a measure as documented and observed evidence, but the degree to which teachers self-report is itself an indication of implementation.

Alignment and articulation of master plan design, champions who coordinate, timelines that build capacity, and progressive expectations for rigor distinguish next-generation school improvement strategies from first generation. If the master plan design includes these components, the school improvement team will be positioned to identify and implement targeted research-based strategies.

Targeted Research-Based Strategies

JANUARY 10, 3:00 P.M. Back at Kelly County High School, every department had agreed to adopt a reading initiative, and the strategies employed were varied and exciting. The visual and fine arts department chose to implement reciprocal teaching, a four-component reading model that engaged students in higher-order thinking processes with writing summaries. The health and physical education team agreed to emphasize text-self connections in every reading or writing assignment to focus kids on what it means to eat well, exercise regularly, and avoid high-risk behaviors. The three English/language arts action steps reinforced these strategies by applying HSPA warm-up drills for self-editing and revision, using AP syllabi to increase rigor in each classroom, and including higher-order thinking activities in lesson planning. The math goal mirrored this process, as explaining reasoning was used to promote higher-order thinking. HSPA warm-up drills worked nicely in both content areas. Everything appeared to be on track when Byron met Yohannon at the country club that unusually warm winter afternoon.

"Thanks for helping me understand the action steps in your plan, Byron. Based on your notes, they clearly represent applied practices from the research. Now help me understand how these strategies will close the achievement gap for special education students."

"Well, the common classroom opening activity will help everyone, but will also provide a defined protocol that IEP students can rely on and master relatively early in the school year. In addition, the common emphases in math and English/language arts help provide the structure needed for most IEP students," Byron explained.

"That makes perfect sense, but I'm still trying to understand how that actually helps special education kids specifically."

"We rely on staff designated to manage each student's special program, and we assume they will make the necessary adjustments."

Yohannon paused, and passed Byron a basket of rolls, "How is that working out?"

In the era of accountability, almost all school improvement teams select research-based strategies, but only a small minority of schools target strategies for specific groups of learners. If a goal is specific enough to describe success that would satisfy the skeptics, the goal will specify the targeted group the improvement will impact. Shouldn't strategies be as targeted as possible to meet student needs? In practice, such precise and explicit strategies become powerful interventions that increase the likelihood of success for all learners (Birman, Reeve, & Sattler, 1998). Let us consider a few pertinent and timely examples.

English Language Learners (ELLs)

Sheltered instruction is a phrase used to describe instructional practices that make content more accessible for ELLs. The Sheltered Instruction Observation Protocol (SIOP) is a well-researched model in which teachers use a thirty-item checklist for lesson planning to link language and content in their instruction, manage their own professional development, and increase their ability to accommodate students at all levels of language acquisition proficiency (Echevarria, Vogt, & Short, 2004). Veteran and expert teachers recognize the SIOP components as effective teaching strategies for *all* students—not just ELLs (Bonnie Bishop, personal communication, July 21, 2008). The SIOP protocol represents a classic targeted research-based strategy that improvement teams need to pursue if they are to achieve next-generation school improvement for all students.

Self-Management Strategies for Asperger's Syndrome

A second example of a targeted research-based strategy is self-management; in this strategy, students are taught to identify and monitor target behaviors for improvement. Most teachers already routinely use elements of self-management, and, once again, a selected strategy for targeted groups of learners almost always has a beneficial impact in terms of instruction for all students.

Response to Intervention (RTI)

Response to intervention is a formal process designed to meet the needs of struggling learners and limit false positive identification of learning disabilities, by proactively designing and implementing interventions early and often for students who need extra support—before eligibility for special education is considered. The process has the added benefit of replacing the discrepancy model of identification for special education with an approach that more accurately connects assessments with the subsequent instruction designed to meet student needs. To many, RTI is a special education issue associated with the mandates of the No Child Left Behind Act (2002). In reality, response to intervention is the most significant change in a generation in terms of how services are provided to struggling students (Gresham, 2001). The RTI process is designed to ensure that local assessments and local skill-based interventions are the driving factors to serve struggling learners. In a meta-analysis of RTI in several states, Wedl and Schroeder (2005) note:

> While educators suggest that "this is what we do," in reality, instructional modification does not occur frequently and typically is not done systematically or based on performance data. At times we try to make students change when it is our instruction that must change. (p. 2)

This statement is a classic illustration of the pitfalls reviewed earlier that prevent and inhibit quality school improvement. Far too often, we assume that best practices are applied with discipline and consistency, while the reality is that many teachers are given multiple fragmented messages and asked to achieve unrealistic expectations; as a result, they experience initiative overload. RTI provides a very powerful protocol that has dramatically reduced the number of students referred to special education, reduced the time to determine eligibility for those ultimately evaluated for placement, and replaced questionable eligibility criteria with local frequent assessments of achievement. Fuchs and Fuchs (2001) describe the basic protocol in the following four components in table 4.1.

Table 4.1: Response to Intervention Protocol

Response to Intervention Protocol	Responsibility
Step 1: Screening	General Education
Step 2: Implementing and Monitoring Classroom Instruction	General Education
Step 3: Implementing and Monitoring Diagnostic Instructional Trials	General and Special Education
Step 4: Assessment and Designation of Learning Disabilities and Special Education Placement	General and Special Education

Fuchs & Fuchs, 2001

The critical change in terms of professional practice that RTI brings to school improvement effort is four-fold: (1) an emphasis on precise identification of instructional strategies based on skill deficits; (2) frequent feedback among professionals; (3) frequent, short-cycle assessments; and (4) frequent monitoring of progress for each student. RTI should be an exemplar for monitoring, as Fuchs and Fuchs recommend weekly monitoring on locally developed short-cycle assessments.

Complexity and Depth

A final example of a targeted research-based strategy is one targeted to gifted and talented learners. Sandra Kaplan developed a model of complexity and depth that includes several strategies designed to engage high-ability and talented students. Her model identifies the following components of depth: (1) simple to abstract content; (2) language of the disciplines, including vocabulary and history of the discipline; (3) details, including gaps and extraneous details; (4) trends and patterns within the content; (5) unanswered questions from text; (6) ethics of the discipline; and (7) big ideas (as cited in Tomlinson et al., 2002). Targeting these strategies to gifted and talented students only enriches instruction for all students.

There is one final practical reason for targeting selected instructional strategies. By so doing, participants in the selection of the strategy wrestle with its design, engage in team dialogue, and promote a local solution that represents the collective wisdom of each team. Anything that can help teams reflect together will facilitate creative, powerful, locally developed strategies. School improvement for the next generation will generate strategies that have yet to be evaluated or published, as school improvement efforts become an incubator for innovation and excellence. As practitioners, we need only insist that we take the time to look for both.

The National Staff Development Council (NSDC) developed a set of standards in 2001 that address the context of professional learning, the process of professional learning, and content standards that address equity, quality of instruction, and family involvement. If the improvement team identifies targeted research-based strategies to meet the needs of specific groups of students, professional development will be essential to achieve the level of proficiency needed to make best practices common practice. Indeed, changing practice without equipping the practitioners is not only an oxymoron, but also a recipe for disappointment and undue stress on professional educators.

Professional Development Focus

The third step in achieving deep implementation is ensuring that professional development is focused, limited in number, and directly aligned with the change initiative content. Many of the thousands of school improvement plans we reviewed include a dozen or more professional development initiatives within a single academic school year. Such plans are patently unrealistic, and we cannot cite a single plan with so many initiatives that resulted in deep implementation with fidelity. That is not to say that schools can't deliver multiple professional development initiatives in a single year. Many schools do so, and some make it look easy. The question that begs an answer, however, is whether that investment in training translates into the kind of improvements in professional practice that can be sustained over time, much less become a self-sustaining component of the school's culture.

The current improvement plan at Kelly County High School was deliberately pared back to only three goals and three primary action strategies. Byron had been persuaded by his administrative team at the end of the previous year that fewer was better, and there was a general acknowledgment that each planned improvement action step needed to be supported by professional development of some kind. The plan, however, was vague about how that would be provided, and while the district language arts coordinator was scheduled to provide training to all departments, the school failed to extend the math initiative (explanation of reasoning) schoolwide. In addition, KCHS's tradition was to allow faculty and departments to opt in rather than have a process to opt out of school improvement when necessary. As a result, the urgency that Byron hoped for was diluted by competing priorities.

Schools, districts, and departments that attempt to accomplish more than time will allow risk diluting their priorities to such an extent that they can't realize the intended benefit of the training. Often, unintended consequences result from attempting to do too much, producing confusion, frustration, and victimization "by initiative overload" (Fullan, 2001b, p. 21). If the professional development is important enough to be included in the schoolwide improvement plan, and important enough to invest time and money for the entire team or faculty to acquire the skills and knowledge associated with it, then the application of such knowledge and skills must be supported with supervision and follow-up. Leaders can demonstrate that focus with reminders, suggestions, and recognition of teacher efforts, or by documenting such efforts in observation and evaluation narratives. Failure to do so will result in indifference and communication that other things are of equal or greater importance.

Professional Development Implementation

JANUARY 15, 2:00 P.M. Joanne, the district language arts coordinator at Kelly County High School, took three weeks off for a Mediterranean cruise that her sister won, allowing her to connect the Thanksgiving and winter holiday breaks. Byron was faced with the absence of a key player from late November until early January. Because of Joanne's lengthy tenure and huge bank of sick and personal days, the district was more than amenable to her taking this once-in-a-lifetime trip. The problem for KCHS was that Joanne was scheduled during both early release days to train departments in a variety of reading/language arts initiatives, including those selected for visual and fine arts, health and physical education, and for science, which chose root word analysis to expand vocabulary. So the trainings were canceled, and, consequently, departments never implemented the reading initiative plan with any consistency.

The district had a very comprehensive teacher induction program, but in the current program, mentors focused on classroom management rather than the reading strategies in English/language arts or the explanation of reasoning in mathematics from KCHS's improvement plan. The math department, however, used every-other department meeting to model explanation of reasoning across course content, and Karen, the department head, reported, "This is the most valuable professional development I have received in years, and all of it from my peers."

Implementation of the improvement plan was contingent on a voluntary effort by staff to implement HSPA warm-up drills and use the AP syllabus to increase rigor in each classroom, but none of the administrators initially looked for these practices in particular, nor did they provide feedback around the school improvement initiatives. To some, implementation seemed nonnegotiable, to others, optional—and the degree to which these practices were institutionalized was not clear by mid-January. The assistant principal, Marilyn, found that less than ten of the forty-seven classroom walkthroughs (CWTs) referenced anything about the improvement plan. These data were particularly discouraging to Byron, as he conducted nine himself and believed his CWTs consistently addressed the plan. Marilyn's data revealed, however, that even Byron only referenced the plan 55 percent of the time.

Providing a limited number of professional development initiatives and ensuring that teachers (and principals) are supported and recognized for applying that training to their leadership or classroom practice is necessary but insufficient in maximizing the degree to which the improvement initiative is translated and sustained in practice. To be effective, professional development needs to be sustained well after the innovation has been introduced. The following attributes define quality professional development in terms of school improvement efforts:

▶ Implementation of specific professional development and research-based strategies

▶ Patient and persistent coaching, as well as mentoring linked to each initiative

▶ Provision of multiple opportunities and deliberate practice for training or retraining to support teachers and build capacity throughout the academic year

▶ Allocation of time, strategies, and resources to reflect adult learning needs (limited initiatives, aligned focused professional development, integrated planning, related support structures, and so on) to sustain growth over time

A major difference between student learners and adult learners is that adults need to see the connection between the professional learning provided and their own personal professional practice. Our time is too precious, our task too daunting to fail to help those individuals implementing new practices understand how they impact their day-to-day work. The premise of professional development implementation is that improvement is accompanied by professional learning that builds capacity, and that adult learners have time to practice that learning as well as time to engage in "reflection-in-action" (Schön, 1987, p. 27). Many schools and school systems have attempted to ratchet up the rigor for students in terms of responding to the higher levels of thinking in Bloom's Taxonomy (Anderson & Krathwohl, 2001), but until all faculty are comfortable engaging in equally challenging levels of thinking, it is unlikely goals about student thinking and metacognition will be achieved.

To sustain professional development, a quality implementation framework includes a system of modeling, mentoring, and coaching. Furthermore, next-generation school improvement will differentiate training to meet people where they are on the learning continuum. Adults, like students, require varying levels of support, time, and practice to acquire and master new knowledge and skills. Figure 4.5 describes how quality implementation distinguished gains in student achievement on the EQAO report for over two hundred schools across Ontario, Canada.

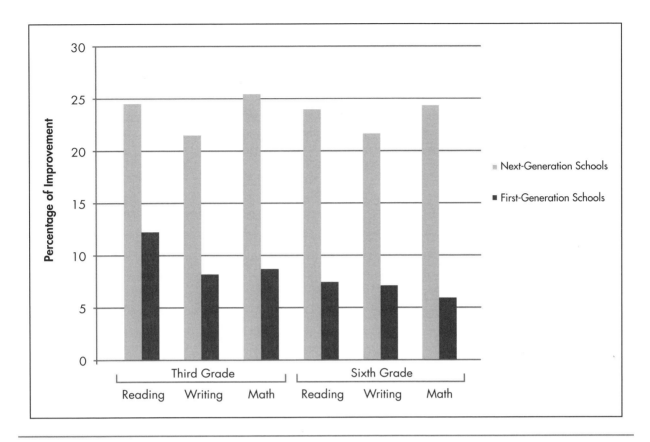

Figure 4.5: Ontario combined achievement gains on the EQAO as a result of professional development implementation 2002–2007.

Leadership and Learning Center, 2008, used with permission

Modeling, mentoring, and coaching are critical components of professional development implementation; these are all strategies to support staff as they attempt to implement new knowledge and skills. Once again, Canadian students from Ontario schools with proficient practices in the implementation of professional development scored significantly higher than their peers in schools that did not demonstrate proficiency in this area.

A necessary corollary to support is deliberate practice—a systematic means to improve current practice. Colvin (2008) examined two endeavors in which cumulative performance is absolutely essential—sports and music—and found that the real distinguishing factor between success and greatness was neither native ability nor intelligence, but rather deliberate, sustained practice. Quality professional development implementation for school improvement should include the following five aspects of deliberate practice:

1. practice should focus on areas of skill deficit in terms of proficiency at modeling the practice

2. practice should be in areas that can be repeated often

3. practice should include both intrinsic and extrinsic feedback

4. practice should be mentally challenging and require mental preplanning and concentration before, during, and after practice

5. practice should require effort (Colvin, 2008, p. 66)

The first aspect merely means that the practice focuses on skill deficits rather than strengths, not unlike the RTI process for students. That is, the professional development implementation step of school improvement plans would describe explicitly the area where practice was needed. A golfing analogy helps illustrate the point. The novice practice often includes selecting one's favorite golf club, then alternating to other shots that are enjoyable. Deliberate practice for professionals, however, includes systematic practice with their weakest golf club, not their favorite. They would repeat the use of their weakest club dozens if not hundreds of times until they mastered the skill and it became automatic. Deliberate practice for educators might involve practicing the design and delivery of a reciprocal teaching lesson and focusing on a weak element such as the questioning component.

The second aspect, repeatability, invites school improvement planners to determine what skill can be practiced deeply enough to master it. An improvement strategy that educators engage in monthly is not apt to provide sufficient practice to master.

Feedback, the third aspect, lends itself to self-assessment, in which performance standards are clearly understood and assessed independently. Deliberate practice feedback is also external, such as feedback from a principal's walkthrough or from a peer observation. Even better, a leader could invite students into the learning process by assigning one student to gather data regularly—let's say, every Thursday at 9:00 a.m.—about the degree to which the strategy is practiced at a proficient level, and/or the degree to which students actually demonstrated the learning (such as by counting the number of times teacher and students used open-ended or higher-order questions). Feedback needs to be as immediate as possible, and if the action step involves teachers applying a particular process of inquiry in science, then feedback needs to come from others as well as a routine self-assessment.

The fourth aspect of deliberate practice is to create structures that challenge students mentally. This is as basic as providing unfamiliar vocabulary to students and asking them to apply their word attack skills (context clues, beginning sounds) to engage in higher levels of reading. Teachers who engage in running records at any level understand the value of this process to challenge students to engage mentally and achieve at higher levels one step at a time.

Because practice should require effort (the fifth aspect), effective teachers are careful to establish conditions to motivate and engage students to pursue new levels of performance. This is particularly evident in cooperative learning where students are obligated to one another and often compete with in-class teams, or when students are provided with support in practice with familiar material but expected to demonstrate the skill unassisted in a different content area. It is important to recognize that each of the five attributes of deliberate practice are interdependent.

School improvement for the next generation will require professional development to be focused and articulated to sustain and extend innovative improvements until such best practices become common for all practitioners. The school improvement process offers a next generation of ideas and structures to respond effectively to the realities of adult learning, unanticipated events, and changes.

Parental Engagement

JANUARY 20, 4:45 P.M. The first few weeks back in school were busy, Byron thought as he shut his door and gazed out his office window, taking stock of the school year thus far. Byron prided himself on having excellent and pervasive parent involvement at KCHS, and viewed his growing relationship with Yohannon as an indicator of his leadership in that area. In fact, KCHS had frequent contact with parents and excellent attendance at back-to-school and teacher conferences. The parent portal within the student information system was used frequently by parents and teachers to track student progress, maintain communication about grades and assignments, and coordinate meeting times for very busy parents. The improvement plan did not reference parent involvement for these reasons.

Carol, the parent representative on the school improvement team, was waiting on the line for Byron. "Byron, I just reviewed our plan, and I was struck by the fact that it doesn't address parent involvement. Given that we have a new student information system, shouldn't we be doing more to engage parents, rather than less?"

"Thanks for calling, Carol, but this year's plan is really all about the instructional response at school," Byron said, "and we needed to limit our strategies."

"Isn't there something I should be doing to help Silas with reading and higher-order thinking skills from home?"

"That's a very good question. I'll put it on our next meeting agenda so we can discuss the issue."

Parental involvement has long been recognized as an antecedent condition for improved student achievement (Epstein & Sheldon, 2002; Lezotte, 2008). A next-generation plan not only defines how information is provided to parents, but also defines training opportunities and how student and school progress will be consistently communicated in ways that are accessible by all parents, in their native language, and at times convenient to their work schedules. Access, education, and transparency are superior indicators of parental engagement than participation on school committees, fundraising, or attendance at school events, and more and more schools offer evening classes to help parents use technology, speak English, and understand standards in math or science. Because of new technologies, there is little excuse to define parental involvement as attendance at school events that occur at times more convenient to the staff than to parents. Improvement plans are particularly effective when a high degree of respect for parents and community members as partners in the educational process is evident in its strategies and action steps.

Final Thoughts

Pfeffer and Sutton (2006) conclude that "even the best change decision will be a disaster if it is implemented poorly" (p. 177). Schools are busy, multifaceted organizations that have a life cycle of their own apart from any school improvement efforts. As a result, only a limited number of opportunities for change exist in any improvement cycle, and wise school leaders will acknowledge the need to sweat the small stuff rather than allowing the urgent to trump the important.

To improve schools so that best practices are sustained over time requires attention to the master plan design, targeted research-based strategies, professional development focus, professional development implementation, and parental engagement. The next generation of school improvement efforts will meet or exceed SMART goals by paying attention to the details of deliberate practice, inviting champions to coordinate areas of their expertise, delineating timelines that build capacity, and creating progressive expectations that increase rigor. Schools will avoid the pitfalls of casual strategy selection or fragmented initiatives when they ascribe responsibility for student achievement to the professional practices we employ. Students and programs matter, but how we deliver and sustain practices is every bit as important as the best practices we select. Chapter 5 introduces us to the next phase of improvement, monitoring. Planning in collaboration and implementing with accountability are necessary components for the next generation of schools, but they are incomplete without monitoring—the critical and powerful phase of measuring the degree of implementation, assessing progress frequently, and providing a means for needed midcourse corrections.

Key Questions for Team Study

Implementation is making sure what needs to get done gets done.
Identify acts of leadership in your school or district that provide assurance. What are the leverage points that move ideas into action?

Champions coordinate, communicate, and chart.
To what degree do you distribute responsibility for completing key action steps? How is assigning one or two individuals to oversee action steps an advantage?

To ensure rigor, plans must be progressive and explicit.
To what degree does your current plan ensure that quality of implementation increases as the improvement cycle unfolds?

Improvement without professional development is an oxymoron.
Discuss this statement with colleagues. Do you agree or disagree? Why?

5 ▶ Monitoring and Midcourse Corrections

Act on the best evidence possible, and learn from your mistakes.

—Robert Sutton

JANUARY 28, 9:00 A.M. With the first semester behind him, Byron tasked two members of his leadership team to cross-tabulate the data about implementing the improvement plans with readily available information about students by subgroup, course offering, attendance, and grades. Kim crunched the numbers, and Marilyn, the assistant principal, indentified queries about teaching practices and learning outcomes. Byron knew that January meetings to launch the second semester—both as small teams and as a faculty—were critical to set the tone for the remainder of the school year, and the brief holiday respite provided him time to make a number of midcourse corrections. Adjustments included:

▶ Beginning second semester, the administrative team would post the outcomes of classroom walkthroughs in terms of the degree to which the action steps for the improvement plan were evident. Charts would examine only observed practices and any correlation with improved student achievement or behavior, not the names of the teachers.

▶ The school improvement plan would be the measure against which administrative decisions would be made about time, opportunity, and resources. Requests for funds that did not align with the school improvement plan would be deferred until the next year.

▶ Faculty meetings would no longer be optional, but two choices would be provided: one before school and the traditional after-school meeting. Most importantly, each meeting gave Byron an opportunity to practice and reinforce the team's "collective commitments"—that is, the agreed-upon ways of interacting with one another to improve KCHS. Each meeting would include a summary of "lessons learned" created by a member of the teaching faculty.

Byron knew the whole world would not change as a result of these alterations, but he also knew KCHS would be better for them. By trial and error, he would discover what worked to improve achievement for those students the school was not reaching, and through a systematic focus on school improvement, those trials and errors would become the basis for savvy data analysis.

Over the course of six months of meetings, Yohannon's probing questions helped Byron begin to see his work and profession in a whole new light. He didn't need to abandon his structure; he needed to reflect on how he spent his time, what he paid attention to, and what he was willing to learn from. The decision was not whether to monitor progress, but how. After discussion, Byron and his staff decided to monitor not only improvements in achievement, but also improvements in practices in terms of curriculum provided, assessments administered, and instruction delivered.

Thomas Edison, the American inventor, is arguably one of the most creative and intelligent individuals of his time, yet history tells us that he attended school in Michigan for only three months before being expelled at the age of twelve because teachers thought he was educationally abnormal. Edison tried and failed over one thousand times to perfect the incandescent electric light bulb, and when advised by his colleagues and friends to give up the whole project because it was doomed to failure, he replied with total conviction and some surprise, "Why, I haven't failed; I've just found a thousand ways in which my formula doesn't work!" His statement, "Genius is 1 percent inspiration and 99 percent perspiration," reveals as much about his method as his tenacity and mental discipline, and his method is very familiar to the physicist who advised KCHS's principal to find success, understand it, and replicate it.

Trial-and-Error Learning

Monitoring determines progress toward achievement of the school's goals and uses feedback to indicate necessary midcourse corrections. At times, monitoring will illustrate that the plan is on track and working, just as in a classroom, checking for understanding may reveal that the students have grasped the instructional content presented in a lesson plan. The process of monitoring culminates in feedback that instructs us about what to do. Feedback that indicates a strategy is not working is just as valuable, in terms of learning, as that which demonstrates a strategy is working as planned. Thus, monitoring examines to see and verify what is happening, and communicates what has been seen to guide adjustments and inform participants.

School improvement efforts are most effective when they create and test many hypotheses regarding student achievement. Like Edison, next-generation school leaders must also be wise enough to continuously "audit their actions" (Kouzes & Posner, 1995, p. 236) by gathering and using data to inform their daily work. If Edison had monitored his experiments the way many school improvement plans are monitored, he would have forsaken his quest long before his breakthrough. Schools often make two common errors: (1) infrequent monitoring and (2) monitoring of compliance. First, it is not uncommon for schools to establish a monitoring schedule that spans the entire school calendar, rather than specifying key points in time. One common outcome of this uncertain timeline is that urgent events hijack planned monitoring of important ongoing work. The more frequent the monitoring, the greater the opportunity to determine what actually contributes to improved student achievement as well as the degree to which there is fidelity of implementation.

Second, the error of compliance is equally common, as many schools monitor adults' initial participation in the initiative (for example, how many teachers attend Marzano's workshop on effective teaching strategies) rather than monitoring their increased precision in use of the initiative (for example, the percentage of faculty applying what they learned in the Marzano workshop at a proficient or higher level). Monitoring the number of staff who attend professional development training is analogous to Edison monitoring the materials he used up in his experiments. Edison ruled out ineffective practices not by tracking quantities of materials, but by tracking the *process* distinctions within the sequences he employed. All too often, schools assume that monitoring attendance or distribution of materials is equivalent to deep and effective implementation. Yohannon recommended to Byron that school improvement efforts be monitored to allow the school to learn from every action step. Monitoring is the ideal vehicle for discovery, because it determines the degree to which sound practices are replicated and ineffective practices are deleted.

Midcourse Corrections

Early coal mines did not feature ventilation systems, so miners would routinely bring a caged canary into new coal seams to serve as early warning systems. Canaries are especially sensitive to methane and carbon monoxide, which makes them ideal for detecting dangerous gas buildups. As long as the canary kept singing, the miners knew their air supply was safe; a dead canary signaled an immediate evacuation. Next-generation school improvement teams use similar early warning systems or "canaries in the schoolhouse" (White, 2005b, p. 38) to detect the health of the working environment. Instead of canaries, educators use information sentinels to help them know whether the organization is in good academic shape. These information warning signs are only possible when effective monitoring strategies are in place; the same applies to early success indicators as well. As Byron discovered, midcourse corrections must be systematic to allow adjustments without major disruptions in the improvement process.

Fullan (1999) emphasizes the importance of establishing collaborative cultures and the work that is required to sustain them. He suggested that "school infrastructures must change and one needed change is the creation of a rigorous accountability system with the capability to scrutinize improvement through monitoring" (p. 53). Schmoker describes monitoring formats that make adjustments without disruptions as "quality reviews" (2006, p. 57). He challenges leaders to facilitate "quarterly curriculum reviews" (p. 130) to verify that essential standards are being taught as well as the degree to which students are learning those standards. To Fullan, monitoring is "one of the most powerful high-leverage strategies to improve student achievement" (1999, p. 71).

One of the pitfalls of annual school improvement planning is that, once written, the plan is rarely, if ever, revisited. A plan with coffee stains and dog-eared pages, by contrast, has visible proof of constant use. Strikethroughs serve as testimonials to deletions and modifications, and comments in the margin provide evidence of ongoing reflection and new learning. Sticky notes of to-do lists attached to various sections remind us that school improvement is a process important enough to record changes as they occur. We need an official record, and we need a process that occurs frequently enough to trigger adjustments (Popham, 2003; Schmoker, 2006). Consequently, a system to amend school improvement plans helps ensure that midcourse corrections are made with agility.

Checking for Understanding

As noted earlier, monitoring is to school improvement what checking for understanding is to classroom teaching. Monitoring offers each school improvement team a series of reality checks, just as checking for understanding allows teachers to adjust lesson plans to meet the needs of their students. Teachers check for understanding when they probe with open-ended questions that invite reflective, thoughtful answers, as opposed to yes/no recall questions. Similarly, monitoring serves as a schoolwide check for understanding when improvement plans probe for understanding about the degree to which the action step has been delivered as designed. Figure 5.1 depicts the dramatic difference in student achievement gains as a function of a quality monitoring plan. Note that student achievement in schools whose monitoring of improvement efforts exceeded the standard (for instance, by monitoring a range of school-based student assessment data as well as adult practice data), based on the use of a common rubric, demonstrated twice the gains of students in "needs improvement" schools (again, based on rubric scores).

The research we conducted in Clark County School District over four years makes it clear that "monitoring is a particularly important variable in influencing student achievement and equity" (Reeves, 2006, p. 70). More importantly, Clark County's results were not an anomaly, as the Houston Independent School District (HISD) experienced similar gains from 2005 to 2007 on the TAKS (see fig. 5.2, page 90).

In HISD, student achievement in schools whose monitoring plans were rated as "exemplary" (based upon a rubric score) demonstrated three times the gains during the two-year period than students who attended schools with a monitoring plan rated as "needs improvement." Both sets of data confirm Fernandez's (2006) finding that the quality of school improvement components were positively related to improved student achievement for statewide norm-referenced assessments.

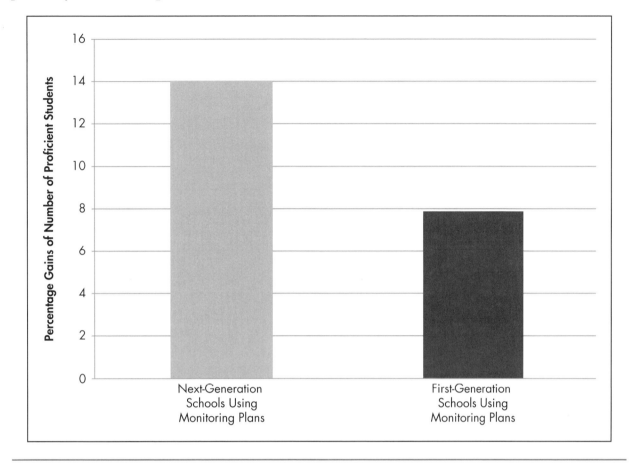

Figure 5.1: Clark County School District achievement gains on the CRT as a result of monitoring plans, 2005–2007.

Reeves et al., 2007, used with permission

Giving Feedback

We know that success for adult learners is in large part a function of meaningful and corrective feedback (Colvin, 2008; Hattie, 1992; Lencioni, 2007; White, 2005b), and quality feedback is both targeted and timely. Feedback as a predictor of success for students is well established (Hattie, 1992; Marzano, 2007), and monitoring provides feedback that drives midcourse corrections. If we are to improve school improvement, then monitoring that action research must be the source of feedback that informs both our instructional and leadership practice. Thus, just as Edison monitored his experiments, found a thousand ways in which his formula didn't work, and pushed through until the formula was right, next-generation school improvement teams who monitor their improvement work will also discover what initial hypotheses didn't work and persist until the improvement "formula" is right.

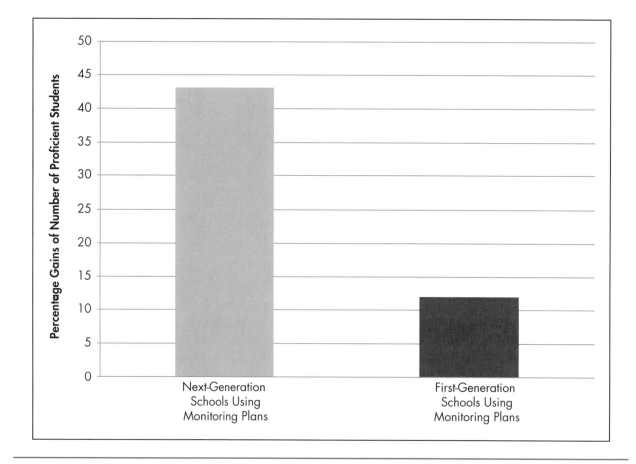

Figure 5.2: Houston ISD achievement gains on TAKS as a result of monitoring, 2005–2007.

Leadership and Learning Center, 2007b, used with permission

Adults and children benefit greatly from receiving feedback that is corrective, timely, and specific regarding the degree to which an initiative is implemented as well as its impact on student achievement (Bransford, Brown, & Cooking, 2000). Feedback from monitoring requires attention to the practical realities of who will do what when, and how trigger mechanisms (midcourse corrections) will transpire to ensure that the school is making adjustments on a few issues that matter over an extended period of time (DuFour et al., 2008).

Monitoring Plan

FEBRUARY, 6, 4:00 P.M. Helen reported that the school improvement team was having a hard time keeping colleagues focused on both the warm-up drills and the use of the AP syllabus. Most elective departments, including world languages and technical education, simply were not doing the warm-up drills, as the content was unfamiliar to their work. Teachers were upfront about their concerns, and department chairs were at a loss to explain why teachers should include them daily. The practice that was almost universal in September was rare by February.

KCHS planned to monitor the use of HSPA warm-up drills that incorporated editing skills, use of open-ended responses, and skill in applying literary terms, but the team failed to specify a monitoring *schedule*, particularly for action steps to establish a reading initiative in all departments. While the plan described the use of the AP syllabi and textbooks, it monitored student achievement instead, a common error of school improvement teams. At KCHS, there was an assumption that all you really need to monitor is student achievement as that will indicate whether efforts are working. That thinking may have been sufficient for the first generation of school improvement, but by monitoring only the outcomes, schools miss the opportunity to determine the degree to which selected practices influence those outcomes. Because the school neglected to measure use of the AP syllabi, they have no means to determine the impact of their selected strategies. School improvement for the next generation intentionally and systematically monitors the initiatives and practices teams select to ensure fidelity of implementation rather than haphazard and variable implementation.

The next generation of monitoring describes explicit data to be monitored; when it will be monitored; and who will be responsible for conducting routine data collection and analysis, and reporting progress toward school improvement goals. The monitoring plan should clearly articulate the type of data to be collected and analyzed. Moreover, monitoring plans must specify a systematic examination of progress in student achievement and in building staff capacity. If Byron and the staff at KCHS had built such a monitoring plan, they would have witnessed a steady monthly increase in the percentage of staff implementing HSPA warm-up drills at the "proficient" or higher levels throughout the school and school year.

Compare the monitoring plans of School A and School B, which we have extracted from work with clients, in table 5.1 (page 92).

Both schools had goals to close achievement gaps in reading for students receiving free and reduced lunch, but which monitoring plan is most apt to be fully implemented? School A describes their strategy in terms of frequency of PLC meetings, while School B relies on an after-school tutorial. School A identifies several persons responsible for monitoring, while School B identifies the instructional coach to coordinate the tutorial data and the English/language arts chair to monitor the modified lessons. Who will ensure that each PLC meeting actually produces any instructional decisions? The answer is obviously unclear from School A's documentation.

In terms of the measurement (assessment) selected, School A identifies everything that will happen in the classrooms, while School B describes a short-cycle assessment every three weeks and delineates expectations for process papers. The timelines also differ dramatically, as School A notes the strategy will happen all year long, while School B describes which days for which weeks, and even schedules time to review the process and make needed midcourse corrections. There is greater clarity in the plan that explicitly identifies what will serve as an indicator of success and when data will be examined, posted, and discussed.

Table 5.1: A Comparison of Monitoring Plans

	Strategy/ Action	Responsible Person	Measurement	Timeline
School A	The sixth-grade PLC will meet weekly to analyze data to establish instructional decisions and interventions.	F. Halderon Principal Science lab teacher Sixth-grade classroom teachers	Weekly teacher-made tests, benchmark tests every three weeks, Central Region Benchmarks, common assessments, rubrics, portfolio reflections, vocabulary development	Aug. 2007–May 2008
School B	All teachers will provide tutorials after school two days per month in each of the core subject areas. Tutorials will be based on common assessment disaggregated data provided the prior week. Schedule will be developed and monitored by department chairs.	Instructional coach will (1) disaggregate tutorial data, post it weekly, and present at faculty meeting each month and (2) guide four modified lessons, one per week for all teachers. English/language arts chair will monitor the percentage of modified lessons completed.	Every third Friday, students take a common assessment. One process paper will be written for each grade level; a minimum of six process papers will be completed per semester.	Tuesday/Thursday tutorials begin Oct. 11–Dec. 11 Review Dec. 18 Jan. 7–Mar. 11, review Mar. 18 Mar. 25–May 14, review May 18

White & Smith, 2006

Although a process of continuous improvement is not easily discernible from this snapshot of School B, it is possible to identify the connections between the tutorial activities and the development of modified lessons based on tutorial data. These connections are not so clear in School A's plan, which describes PLC meetings as a strategy. School A's measurements are broadly defined, and the action to "establish instructional decisions and interventions" is obtuse. Ironically, School A may have selected the more powerful intervention, but School B has developed a monitoring plan that reveals with greater clarity what they hope to accomplish.

Elkhart Community Schools in Indiana provide an excellent example of a districtwide monitoring system. In 2005, the district began an aggressive staff development program for all teachers and administrators. Leaders selected three related content areas for widespread training: Making Standards Work, data teams, and utilization of Marzano's (2001) effective teaching strategies. Unlike many districts, Elkhart realized that without ongoing coaching and embedded just-in-time training, deep implementation would be difficult to achieve, and even more difficult to sustain. Consequently, Elkhart constructed a monitoring plan to measure the degree to which these practices were implemented, thereby helping administrators "keep a hand on the pulse of change" (Hall & Hord, 2006, p. 192). Elkhart applied progressively rigorous expectations by asking principals to provide evidence of implementation at a defined level of proficiency or higher. The district then asked principals to summarize and present the ongoing results of their implementation efforts at the principals' regularly scheduled monthly meeting. Monitoring was systematic and frequent, and midcourse corrections were provided districtwide. Appendix A provides a sample of the configuration map or scoring guide (pages 151–152) used to measure these important adult practices.

Monitoring Frequency

FEBRUARY 13, NOON. The country club was crowded during the lunch hour as Byron and Yohannon leaned over their table talking. "Our plan uses a variety of assessments, including the district's benchmark tests (administered three times a year for core subjects), departmental common assessments such as the biology final, observation data from CWTs . . ." Byron was about to list more elements of the plan when Yohannon interrupted him.

"Sorry, but what is a CWT?"

"Classroom walkthroughs are brief, seven-minute observations of teaching practices we use to provide same-day corrective feedback to classroom teachers whose class we observe," Byron explained.

"What can you see in just seven minutes?"

Byron smiled, realizing that the brilliant scientist didn't really "get" the business of education, at least in some ways. "We can observe evidence of certain strategies, level of engagement between teacher and students, questioning techniques, alignment with curriculum and lesson plans—all kinds of things."

"What do you measure in these CWTs?"

"We monitor the frequency with which teachers employ selected strategies, the demonstration of observable 'proficient' practices as they apply them, and the presence of predetermined best practices."

"OK, I think I get it. Now, how frequently are these things monitored?"

"Marilyn developed a schedule for all five administrators," Byron said. "We're in classrooms weekly."

Yohannon flipped through the papers on the table. "Where do I find that schedule in your plan?"

Byron looked a little surprised. "Well, we made that change midyear."

Yohannon nodded. "Our monitoring schedules change all the time as well, and we have found that more frequent monitoring is better than less frequent monitoring. What does the educational research say about that?"

"I'm not sure; I do know I don't want to burden my staff unnecessarily."

The monitoring plan must identify the frequency with which progress toward achieving goals will be monitored. Research in both industry and education clearly demonstrates the importance of frequent monitoring and its positive impact on the achievement of ambitious goals (Hattie, 1992; Lezotte, 2008; Reeves, 2009a; Sammons, Hillman, & Mortimore, 1995; Pfeffer & Sutton, 2006; Yeh, 2007). Byron was concerned that frequent monitoring would tax his staff, but the evidence is very strong that monitoring as a means of providing feedback is strongly correlated with improved performance for both adults and students. Consequently, the next generation of monitoring plans monitors all key steps frequently (no less than five to ten times annually), so that there are ample opportunities to make midcourse adjustments when needed. Frequent monitoring allows schools to respond to the difficulties that arise with any implementation endeavor. Such monitoring also directs teams to take actions informed by the data being collected.

KCHS's initial monitoring effort left to chance the frequency for monitoring warm-up drills, revising and editing skills, and open-ended responses using literary terms. Explicit monitoring schedules assist practitioners in the review of teaching, leadership practices, and student performance by establishing dates or weeks in which each monitoring activity will occur and communicating with clarity an expectation of excellence. Table 5.2 compares monitoring frequency to illustrate the value of explicit monitoring.

Table 5.2: Monitoring Frequency Comparison

	Strategy/Action	Responsible Person	Measurement	Timeline
School C	Students will receive instruction based on district power indicators and benchmarks.	Administration Department chairs Grade-level departments All teachers	Common lesson plans Common unit assessments Common content vocabulary FOSL walk data	Weekly, Aug.–May
School D	All students will participate in a specific reading initiative, such as Accelerated Reader, and read twenty minutes each day.	Literacy coach and librarian	Students' nine-week assessment Accelerated Reader scores Reading logs TAKS	2009–2010 school year

White & Smith, 2006

School C reports weekly monitoring (timeline), while School D only specifies that the action step will be monitored throughout the school year. Indicating that monitoring will happen weekly is of little value, though, if it is unclear what will be monitored. In School C, the plan is to monitor the degree to which lesson plans are based on power indicators, but nowhere is that defined. School C also ascribes responsibility for monitoring to virtually everyone. Responsibility for monitoring is not the same as responsibility for implementing, and for that reason, it is recommended that one person be given the opportunity to coordinate the monitoring process and ensure it is completed as designed.

School D has its own challenges, as it plans to monitor the action step throughout the school year. As noted earlier, monitoring schedules that span lengthy periods of time rather than specify precise dates inevitably lead to less-frequent monitoring. School D does, however, have a more precise action step that clearly describes what is intended (participation in a specific reading initiative)—something that can at least be monitored. School D also has wisely assigned the responsibility to champion the action step to the librarian and the literacy coach, individuals who can hold each other accountable for tasks as well as divide the responsibilities clearly (a literacy coach might analyze the assessments, while a librarian might monitor participation in Accelerated Reader). Neither school meets the standard for monitoring frequency, but School D's plan could improve to standard if the timeline for monitoring was made more frequent and more explicit. For both schools, monitoring represents a missed opportunity.

Leadership in Monitoring

Marzano, Waters, and McNulty's (2005) highly influential meta-analysis of leadership supports the leadership obligation to monitor school improvement efforts. They identified twenty-one research-based responsibilities for school principals, including monitoring and evaluation. Monitoring provides the evidence to verify additional leadership responsibilities such as affirmation, communication, input, and intellectual stimulation. Monitoring with feedback is a critical leadership practice that promotes improved student achievement (Schmoker, 2006). The following example illustrates how a simple change in the monitoring structure helped distribute leadership in Hillsboro, Oregon.

The Hillsboro School District redesigned its planning template to influence and shape how school leaders looked at the improvement process. Leaders in this district were determined to influence the thinking of principals and improvement teams to increase specificity and clarity of items monitored (adult cause and student effect data) in order to promote more frequent and informative monitoring of targeted improvement efforts, as illustrated in table 5.3 (page 96). Hillsboro uses the three-tier method found in *Accountability in Action* (Reeves, 2004b), in which Tier I represents districtwide measures such as quarterly benchmarks, attendance, or performance on state assessments; Tier II refers to school and classroom level measures (common formative assessments or the number of classroom walkthroughs conducted); and Tier III refers to a narrative explanation of results. The Xs in table 5.3 indicate in which months each source of data is monitored.

Table 5.3: Hillsboro, Oregon, Monitoring Plan Template

Tier II Indicator(s)	Responsible Person	Source of Data	A	S	O	N	D	J	F	M	A	M
Increase the percentage of teachers who write and implement prescriptive lessons tailored toward the development of successful writing strategies.	Department coordinators and teachers	The percent of self-reported weekly lesson plans that use writing strategies (for instance, three out of four weeks, or one out of four weeks) The percent of classrooms observed using formal writing strategies during CWTs		X	X	X	X	X	X	X	X	X
Increase the percentage of teachers who use Sheltered Instruction Observation Protocol (SIOP) methods in lesson planning.	Principal, ESL Department coordinator, and selected teachers	The percent of self-reported use of SIOP daily The percent of actual use of SIOP methods observed during in CWTs		X	X	X	X	X	X	X	X	X
Begin a data team consisting of teachers who regularly review available information on writing related to best practices and improvement of student learning.	Principal, data team leader, and data team members	Data team leader and data team training Data team meeting minutes		X	X	X	X	X	X	X	X	X

Adapted from *Poynter Middle School, 2006*

Not only does the Hillsboro template require monthly monitoring, it provides even greater clarity by having teachers self-report daily (SIOP) as well as monitor lesson plans weekly; both of these approaches are then verified by the classroom walkthroughs. When leaders specify what will be monitored by whom, celebrate when it occurs, and provide opportunity to make needed midcourse adjustments, their actions serve to build consensus around the value of monitoring as a means to track performance and provide instructive feedback. Leaders need not do all the monitoring, but they need to explicitly describe expectations of how it will occur and what will be done with the data collected.

Leadership in monitoring requires courage, not only to monitor results, but also to negotiate change.

Courage to Monitor

Monitoring the performance of others is a delicate issue for schools, particularly in light of the loosely coupled cultures most educators find themselves in. Schmoker (2006) challenges the profession to create schools "better than anything we've ever seen or imagined" (p. 2) by inviting leaders to have the "courage to monitor" (p. 129) the previously private and protected realm of teaching. He suggests that leaders regularly schedule brief meetings, no more than fifteen to twenty minutes in length, with teacher teams to:

▶ Check whether the essential learning outcomes are being taught

▶ Use results from common formative assessments to determine how consistently such assessments are consulted to guide instruction

▶ Create quarterly curriculum reviews in which teachers showcase the formative assessments they are using along with their results (including samples of student work)

Similarly, central office staff would be wise to conduct comparable reviews with principals, a standard practice of several champion districts showcased throughout this book.

An example of having the courage to monitor is unmistakable at Garden City Elementary in Indianapolis, Indiana. Principal Nicole Law enlisted her leadership team to create an implementation rubric and walkthrough form to monitor key attributes of school improvement; very explicit corrective feedback would be offered virtually every day. Law monitors the degree to which she provides same-day feedback from these walkthroughs, and her intent is always to provide corrective feedback. "I have learned from feedback I have personally received as it helps me see my own blind spots, so I systematically praise people for their strengths," she notes, "but my faculty knows I am going to suggest something to stretch them or suggest resources they need to access to get better, to improve" (personal communication, January 17, 2009). Law's grid covers six domains in instruction—intervention, data analysis, math, writing, guided reading, and physical environment—and every staff member is familiar with each expectation. Figure 5.3 (page 98) offers a slice of Garden City's implementation rubric in which *four* represents deep implementation and *one* represents very little implementation. Law estimates over one hundred classroom walkthroughs with same-day feedback are provided for teachers every month.

Guided Reading/Writing	Mathematics	Data Analysis
Mini-lessons are taught. 4 3 2 1	Conceptual units are developed. 4 3 2 1	Grouping is based on assessment data. 4 3 2 1
Assessment is 1:1; records are run daily. 4 3 2 1	Written responses are part of math units. 4 3 2 1	Data is displayed via easy-to-read graphs. 4 3 2 1
Students independently work on higher-order thinking. 4 3 2 1	Students use technology to demonstrate understanding. 4 3 2 1	Evidence shows that students track data. 4 3 2 1

Figure 5.3: Garden City implementation grid—sample items.

Garden City Elementary, 2009, used with permission

Negotiating Change

Gene Hall and Shirley Hord (2006) find that monitoring is a critical phase in facilitating organizational change, another key leadership responsibility. They reinforce the critical need for practitioners to lead change in five discrete ways:

1. Leaders should monitor change efforts to support implementation at high levels and assess the degree to which school practices are having an impact on student achievement.

2. Leaders need to provide individualized support so that those implementing the intended change become skilled experts over time.

3. Leaders must anticipate and facilitate change at the individual level since "organizations do not change until individuals within it change" (p. 7).

4. Leaders facilitate individuals and organizations as they "move across the implementation bridge" (p. 10) because implementers of innovations don't all learn at the same time or the same rate.

5. Leaders address the concerns of implementers to "reduce resistance to change" (p. 13), thereby increasing the rate of adoption of the innovation.

To influence the change process, monitoring needs to be a collaborative process that is all about improvement and nothing about evaluating individual performance. Monitoring is also about paying attention to the granular and incremental issues involved with implementing any change in practice. Those who sweat the small stuff and pay attention to future change efforts will be more successful if they acknowledge and act upon these principles of effective monitoring.

Final Thoughts

During the first generation of school improvement, monitoring was assumed to occur as needed, and the schedule for monitoring progress was typically described as "yearlong," "September–June," or the "2010–2011 school year" (as in School D). Unless a more precise schedule is in place, the urgent demands on principals inevitably trump the important but nonurgent work of school improvement. Frequent monitoring allows schools to make the same kind of nimble and responsive adjustments for schools that the most effective teachers make within their classrooms (Marzano, 2007; Yeh, 2007).

We have seen how important a cohesive monitoring plan is to school improvement leaders, especially a plan that details frequent monitoring and confirms the need to act on those data by applying midcourse corrections. Next-generation teams monitor teaching and leadership practices that improve the school's capacity to deliver best practices schoolwide, as well as progressive gains in student achievement. They monitor key indicators frequently enough to establish trends and recognize patterns in student learning, and determine professional acquisition and application of knowledge and skills. The best monitoring plans schedule opportunities for midcourse corrections and routine reflection about the school improvement effort.

The extensive research related to this key phase of school improvement teaches us to be mindful of three fundamental concepts: (1) it is essential that monitoring schedules track the "right work" (Elmore, 2004, p. 9) and maintain a record of their efforts for both achievement and professional practice, (2) scheduled monitoring of the right work must be frequent enough (five to ten times per year) to facilitate learning for adults and students as a tool for ongoing improvement, and (3) school improvement teams must commit themselves to just-in-time learning and alter practices based on the evidence they receive. Chapter 6 addresses the final link of the continuous improvement cycle—the evaluation cycle.

Key Questions for Team Study

Monitoring seeks out and uses feedback about the school's progress.
How will school improvement teams build next-generation monitoring systems? How will they differ from current practice?

Monitoring frequency is associated with gains in student achievement.
Why is it beneficial for schools to monitor their improvement efforts more rather than less frequently?

Effective school improvement teams monitor both student achievement and the professional practices that promote or predict that achievement.
Why is it necessary to monitor both achievement and professional practice simultaneously?

For feedback to be useful it must be used.
Are school practitioners at your school learning on the basis of feedback from practice? Should instructional and leadership strategies be altered based on feedback from practice?

6 ▶ Evaluation: Lessons Learned and Next Steps

When people come together to deal with practical problems, it's important for them to consider what they want to create, not just what they want to fix.

—*Peter Senge*

MARCH 20, 9:00 A.M. Byron began to recognize some key lessons he could advance in next year's improvement plan. He was quite skilled at discerning when and how to invite his team, his faculty, and his community into important discussions. He also was skilled at giving away both responsibility and credit for accomplishments, and was recognized by his peers for his understanding of collaboration around the right work and its benefits.

After they'd finished their breakfasts, Yohannon leaned forward, asking, "As you reflect on your improvement process, what have you learned so far this year?"

"For once, I anticipated your question!" Byron laughed. "I think we need to gather data around the context of learning, including time, opportunity, how decisions are made, the degree to which implementation occurs, and how feedback is provided and how often. I have to admit, I hadn't thought of the improvement process in terms of measuring and monitoring what we modify."

"Have you thought about how you would structure the process differently for next year?"

___

Monitoring has been recognized as an important aspect of school improvement, even though school improvement plans from every region of the United States and Canada often describe monitoring with timelines such as "ongoing" or "yearlong." Evaluation, on the other hand, is rarely addressed as anything other than reporting results in terms of goal attainment. Monitoring informs us of the degree to which the plan is working, while evaluation is the process of making meaning of the entire effort, and making decisions about what is working and what is not. This chapter introduces evaluation as a process of learning and decision making, which, like monitoring, impacts every aspect of school improvement.

We noted in chapter 1 that reporting is not evaluating. Instead, next-generation school improvement uses the evaluation cycle to determine the efficiency of the improvement efforts, the degree to which student learning was impacted, and the effectiveness of the changes in terms of capacity building. School improvement templates should plan for reflection and analysis of results following completion of each improvement cycle. One plausible explanation for the limited emphasis on the evaluation cycle is the front-end design of first-generation school improvement efforts; at year's end, the review of the results tends to be rushed.

Since NCLB, there has been an increase in attention to the evaluation process (Engelmann & Engelmann, 2004; Elmore, 2004; Hopkins & West, 2002). David Hopkins and Mel West (2002) suggest that real school improvement will only succeed if evaluation becomes the central focus and tenet of every initiative and improvement effort. The National Study of School Evaluation (NSSE) described evaluation as a process to document the impact of and sustain commitment to continuous improvement (2003). Impact was examined in two ways: (1) achievement gains for students and (2) improvement for the school or school system in terms of instructional or organizational effectiveness. Elmore added to this definition by emphasizing the reciprocal relationship between student performance as an outcome of school improvement and support to build capacity to deliver improved performance (2007). A quality evaluation process must examine the impact of the school improvement effort on achievement and on the school's capacity to introduce, establish, and sustain needed changes in practice.

Attributes of Next-Generation Evaluation

Evaluation is the final phase in a cycle of continuous improvement. Four steps in achieving proficient next-generation evaluation are: (1) comparing planned and actual outcomes; (2) identifying lessons learned with clarity and specificity; (3) applying those lessons to future plans; and

(4) ensuring transparency. These steps are practical and easy to recognize but rarely seen in first-generation school improvement documents.

Tom Guskey and Joellen Killion independently described evaluation in three broad categories in reference to professional development: planning evaluation, formative evaluation, and summative evaluation (as cited in Libby, Piper, & Sandbothe, 2005). This informs our understanding of the evaluation of school improvement efforts by examining impact on student learning, success in terms of capacity building, and lessons to apply in the future. Evaluation should study the degree to which the needs assessed are comprehensive, whether the process of inquiry narrows the focus to generate hypotheses for meaningful change, and whether goals clarify and focus expectations for improvement.

Guskey (2002) describes how the evaluation process should be deliberate and able to determine—through a series of questions about resources, strategies, and perceptions—whether the improvement effort has made a difference. For our purposes, the process boils down to a set of decision options: should the practice be continued, modified, expanded, or discarded? Deliberate evaluation means gathering data throughout the school improvement calendar to be able to answer those basic questions with confidence.

A casual response in school improvement evaluation is similar to a casual selection of instructional strategies (chapter 4), in which the most visible attribute of a best practice is selected rather than the most important. For example, teachers may be familiar and comfortable with a current approach to literacy, even though its effectiveness for the targeted student population is limited. Rather than replacing or modifying the practice, the team often chooses to continue the strategy for one more year because "we need to give it more time." They may be accurate in that assessment, but the evidence about change suggests that when the interventions are sufficiently focused and well articulated, many important changes actually occur very rapidly (Pfeffer & Sutton, 2006; Reeves, 2003; Schmoker, 2001). Giving things more time *gives away* more time.

To avoid the trap of selecting the decision option casually, we adapted Lipton and Wellman's (2001) mentoring framework that guides participants to move from the abstract to the explicit as they gather information: recollections and impressions, supporting factors, similarities and differences, cause-and-effect relationships, and connections. The process begins with a general question about one's impressions: "What comes to your mind when you think of this year's school improvement process?" It also ensures that reviewers examine the evidence. Our approach to evaluation is augmented by Douglas Reeves' (2004b) accountability framework; we consider how achievement data and professional practice (antecedents) interact to consider "the rest of the story." Evaluation of school improvement needs to blend the formative evaluation process, which examines granular aspects of implementation and process outcomes, with traditional summative evaluation, which examines the final results. We now examine evaluation as a formative process, in which decisions are made on the basis of existing evidence to make decisions and changes within the school improvement cycle.

Formative Evaluation: Improving Procedures and Practice

Formative evaluation helps determine whether the program is implemented as designed, whether feedback is provided as planned, and whether midcourse corrections are made in a timely and focused manner. A *summative* evaluation, on the other hand, involves an external, independent review process that gathers evidence of a program's performance and impact. To learn more about the function of formative evaluation, we return to KCHS just before spring break.

APRIL 2, 7:15 A.M. "Byron, could I speak with you for a moment?"

"Of course, Sue, come in." Byron walked around his desk to welcome the chair of the visual arts department. "Please sit down."

Sue pulled out her notes from her department meeting and began, "As you know, we chose to implement reciprocal teaching—a four-part reading model that engaged students in higher-order thinking processes with writing summaries at least weekly. We wanted to use that reflection opportunity to help kids integrate the concepts of line and space and better understand the influence of history on art and the influence of art on history. The idea was well received, but my team has really struggled with making sure the reciprocal teaching sequence is delivered, and I am clueless as to how to gather data on it. When Elsa describes what she is doing in watercolors, and Ed describes reciprocal teaching in oils, they just are not the same strategy. Do you have any ideas?"

Byron smiled. "Sue, you have never ignored a single expectation from this office or from your colleagues, and believe me, the team is very cognizant of how visual arts has been creative—no pun intended!—each and every year. Have you spoken with Joanne or Helen about reciprocal teaching?"

"Joanne referred me to some websites, but translating that into consistent application in my department is something else altogether," Sue replied.

"I wonder if your team needs to have reciprocal teaching modeled, followed by practice and feedback from peers. I'm happy to free up enough money so every visual arts instructor can observe a peer and be observed. Would anything else help?"

"We need more training. I think I can get my team to stay late on Tuesdays for a couple of hours, if you can stipend them and get Helen or Joanne to provide us a refresher on reciprocal teaching. That would take care of the modeling part," Sue added.

Byron offered Sue his hand. "You don't need those lists you bring in. You are fully capable of making your case and leaving this office with everything you need. Come to think of it, you have been doing this for years!" They both laughed, and the smile on Sue's face indicated to Byron that she was more than satisfied with his help. As she left his office, he realized he was helping Sue like Yohannon was helping him.

Sue's attention to the details of how the visual arts department implements the plan is a good example of the formative aspect of evaluation and the leadership required. As a department leader, Sue's concern with the quality of implementation helped her discover where and how to shore up her efforts.

The evaluation process describes effective key attributes within the school improvement plan itself. This framework adapts Guskey's (2002) approach to evaluating professional development, applies the work of Lipton and Wellman (2002) on mentoring, and incorporates the commonsense elements of Douglas Reeves' (2004b) work on accountability. School improvement evaluation needs to focus on finding what works and refining it to work more effectively. It is a key piece to the educational research puzzle that allows success in terms of student achievement to serve as the constant of school improvement. Like our physicist notes, identification of effective practices and elimination of less effective practices is nothing more than pursuit of continuous improvement—a trial-and-error process educators need to understand and embrace. Ben Davis High School in Indianapolis, Indiana, provides a unique example of formative evaluation in the following section.

Comparing Planned Outcomes to Actual Outcomes

Ben Davis High School examined anticipated changes in behavior to provide data to make decisions about school improvement throughout the school year (see table 6.1, page 106). The process focused teachers on looking for and recognizing changes in behaviors and practices associated with the plan and served as a barometer of effectiveness. Because they had clearly delineated planned outcomes, the teachers could compare the actual outcomes in a helpful, insightful way.

By examining knowledge, attitude, and skills, Ben Davis High School found indicators of success at various junctures during the school improvement calendar, which helped them evaluate the impact of their efforts and make the appropriate decisions throughout the school year.

Identifying Lessons Learned

Formative evaluation efforts differ from monitoring only in respect to the decision making involved. As mentioned previously, Guskey (2002) offers four possible conclusions: should the improvement effort be continued, continued with modifications, expanded, or discontinued? Evaluation assumes that one of the four options will ensue as a result of the evidence provided.

The school improvement plan needs to be managed to be implemented deeply, but it must also be responsive to changes identified through the monitoring process. Many of the innovations in schools occur in small incremental improvements that teachers or teacher teams bring to their craft. By constantly monitoring and evaluating the effect—especially of midcourse correction changes—schools are able to identify the practices that contribute to increased success for students.

Table 6.1: Anticipated Changes in Knowledge, Attitude, and Skills as a Result of Implementing Project-Based Learning

Project-Based Learning		
	Students	**Staff/Teacher**	**Stakeholders/ Leadership Team**
Knowledge	Students will take ownership and responsibility for their learning. Students will know: What project-based learning is Steps to long-term projects How to evaluate progress Their learning strengths	How to ask essential "big-idea" questions How to create and use rubrics How to differentiate the learning How to facilitate the classroom lesson and empower student ownership How to create a student-centered learning environment	How to ask essential "big-idea" questions How to create and use rubrics How to differentiate the learning How to facilitate the classroom lesson and empower student ownership How to create a student-centered learning environment How to train, support, and monitor project-based learning
Attitudes	Students believe that individualized, option-driven experiential learning is fun.	We believe that all students have strengths and gifts that can be revealed through relevant experiential learning We believe that project-based learning rekindles teachers' passion for the classroom by encouraging creativity and exciting lesson planning.	We believe that all students have strengths and gifts that can be revealed through relevant experiential learning We believe that project-based learning engages students and focuses teacher energies by encouraging creativity and exciting lesson planning.
Skills	Problem solving Project design and organization Project management Collaboration Presentation Research Communication	Teach, model, inspire, and expect: Problem solving Collaboration Presentation Research Communication Rubrics, grading practices, assessment	Teach, model, inspire, expect, train, support, and monitor: Problem solving Collaboration Presentation Research Communication

Ben Davis High School, 2009, used with permission

Formative evaluation also examines the effectiveness of the school improvement effort by asking specific, directed questions: How successful was the inquiry process in prioritizing goals or generating hypotheses? To what degree were SMART goals timely in terms of set dates for monitoring? Did the master plan design provide parents with convenient meeting times and interpreters in their native language? Formative evaluation of school improvement need not wait for achievement scores to determine whether the plan is working; in many states, summative achievement data isn't provided until late summer or early fall of the subsequent school year, which underscores the need for an evaluation process that is both formative and summative.

Summative Evaluation: Making Meaning of Results

While formative evaluation improves procedures and practices, summative evaluation makes meaning of the results. Summative evaluation also answers the question, "What decision is warranted about the improvement effort?" The four options (continue, modify, discontinue, expand) form the base of an overall evaluation of school improvement.

The sample scoring rubric from the Leadership and Learning Center PIM rubric (appendix A, pages 145–148), is an example of a tool used primarily as a summative evaluation of the overall impact on student achievement, though the criteria for proficiency have been found to be consistent predictors of improved achievement. The rubrics allow schools to examine capacity building and effectiveness by comparing current levels of implementation against these criteria for proficiency. Use of proven tools to assess progress in terms of school improvement functions offers educators the ability to make informed judgments about the effectiveness of improvement aspects and adjust accordingly.

School improvement encompasses a broad spectrum of practices that need to be evaluated in terms of their relative impact on student achievement. The phases of school improvement may themselves have as much bearing on student achievement gains as selected strategies or instructional programs. Our research consistently reveals that schools using monitoring, comprehensive needs assessment, or SMART goals yield greater achievement gains than schools that do not.

Figure 6.1 (page 108) compares achievement levels for Clark County schools that exceeded the rubric standard for a school improvement evaluation cycle with levels for schools that did not meet standard.

Figure 6.2 (page 109) depicts a similar relationship between evaluation and achievement gains on the TAKS in Houston ISD. While by no means conclusive, there is a growing recognition that quality evaluation of school improvement is itself an antecedent condition of achievement gains.

By applying a precise rubric to the school improvement elements within planning, implementation, monitoring, and evaluation, we have been able to isolate a broad range of variables and identify a number of antecedent leadership actions for school improvement. The components included in the next generation of school improvement will assist educational leaders to identify these antecedents of excellence. Just as the body of knowledge and research about teaching and learning has expanded exponentially, a more precise understanding of what works will generate clarity around best practices in school improvement for the next generation.

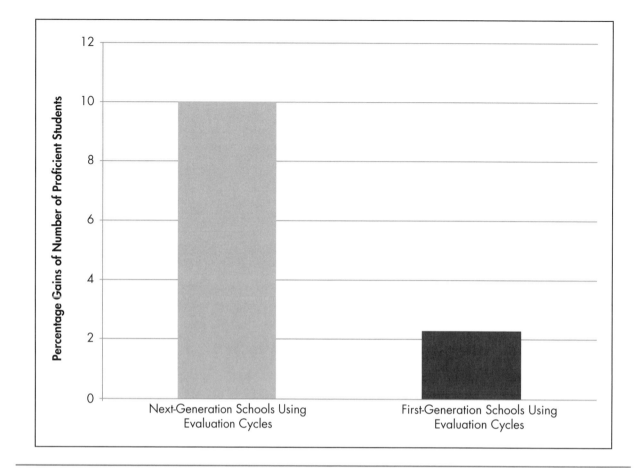

Figure 6.1: Clark County School District achievement gains on the CRT and HSPE as a result of evaluation, 2004–2007.

Reeves et al., 2007, used with permission

What would it mean to student achievement, the elimination of achievement gaps, gradua-tion rates, or retention rates for early-career teachers if schools across the globe would make one improvement in terms of teaching strategies that can be applied across content areas in every classroom?

Applying Lessons to Future Plans

Summative evaluation of school improvement occurs at the end of each improvement cycle, but few school systems deliberately schedule time to reflect on the results. Exemplars that anticipate a thorough evaluation process are provided in appendix A (Hillsboro, Oregon, page 149; Hawthorn, Illinois, page 150). Hillsboro's process clearly contrasts planned results (goals) with actual results achieved, and specifies lessons learned and how they will be applied in the next year's improvement plan. Hawthorn uses language identical to Hillsboro, but highlights those parts of the plan that will be completed at the end of the improvement cycle, leaving white space to indicate areas that need to inform the next planning phase. Hawthorn also borrowed Metropolitan School District of Wayne Township's description of the knowledge, attitudes, and skills that are anticipated to result from a successful improvement effort. All three districts represent the next generation of school improvement efforts that make meaning out of every event and strategy employed in school improvement.

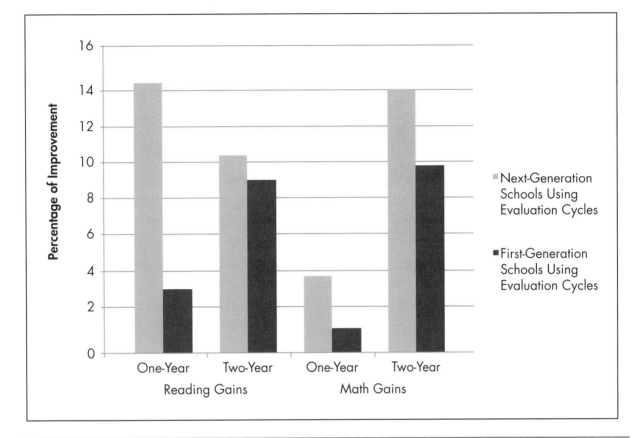

Figure 6.2: Houston ISD achievement gains on TAKS as a result of school evaluation cycles, 2006–2007.

Leadership and Learning Center, 2007b, used with permission

Ensuring Transparency

More importantly, a next-generation evaluation process informs the next year's comprehensive needs assessment and populates it with insights and data about teaching, learning, and leading, all of which need to be shared with everyone involved. Gains and declines in school improvement goals must be communicated without delay to families, educators, staff, patrons, partners, and the public. Many champion school systems have extraordinary levels of transparency in reporting to primary stakeholders. Lisa Lantrip, assistant superintendent for the MSD of Wayne Township, reports,

> We have worked very hard to make our schools welcoming and respectful places for our students' first teachers. School improvement teams understand the importance of transparency, not only in terms of communicating status of school improvement goals but in terms of celebrating incremental gains through data walls

throughout the corporation. Our annual "Data Science Fair" is well publicized and open to the public, and I am pleased to report that parents look forward to it every year. (personal communication, January 13, 2009)

An effective, transparent evaluation cycle communicates what lessons were learned and how they will be applied to future school improvement cycles through newsletters, committee meetings, the Internet, email correspondence, and public displays that both celebrate gains and point out shortcomings.

Leadership and the Evaluation of School Improvement

Leadership is needed to make sure school improvement is evaluated and to make sure that the decisions regarding programs and structures are sound and informed by evidence. The authors have witnessed far too many instances when the urgency of closing school in the spring results in a hurried review of school improvement or no review at all. All too frequently, school improvement plans continue previous efforts or change content areas of focus without the needed reflection to improve. This section offers three areas where leadership is sorely needed to achieve next-generation results: (1) evaluation as vision, (2) evaluation as a way of thinking, and (3) evaluation as venture capital for ideas.

Evaluation as Vision

As we have seen, paradoxically, the final phase in the next-generation school improvement cycle is also the first phase in the next cycle. Improvement thus becomes continuous. Evaluation should inform the comprehensive needs assessment, and a quality evaluation process will require reflection and insight to recognize and identify those lessons that will actually improve future conditions for success. It will certainly require analysis of the data that are gathered through the monitoring process, and it will examine data about capacity building, cost and benefits in terms of time and resources, satisfaction, and the impact of the current effort on the school (or district) culture and operating procedures. Evaluation as vision also will take time to celebrate gains achieved and compare actual achievement to that which was planned. Vision requires us to understand the complexity of the educational process and the "rest of the story" before answering evaluation's essential questions. The end result will be specific lessons learned and specific recommendations for next steps.

Evaluation as a Way of Thinking

Evaluation is not something that can be turned on at the end of the school year. First-generation improvement plans mistake reporting of results as evaluation, a clear indication that evaluation is viewed as a separate activity rather than as a part of an interlinked, seamless process of improvement. Evaluation is all about making meaning and ascribing value, a process that requires both dispassionate reflection and practice weighing evidence from multiple perspectives. When data teams or professional learning communities experience the need to weigh evidence and make decisions based on available data, the practice of evaluating information effectively and developing a degree of collective wisdom is advanced. Schools are designing school improvement for the next generation when they insist that routine meetings conclude with a team member synthesizing the learning that occurred and delineating the plans for next steps. The quality reviews noted in chapter 5 also foster evaluation as a way of thinking as schools deliberately include opportunities for midcourse corrections within their school improvement plan.

Consider Concord Community Schools in Concord, Indiana, where Assistant Superintendent Wayne Stubbs has led the effort to institutionalize data teams as the core strategy for school improvement. A team of junior high math teachers gathered data, analyzed student learning styles, developed a SMART goal, and assessed progress; then they took time to reflect on lessons learned.

> One team member, Dan, noted, "I think we learned that checklists don't work as a strategy for understanding equivalency."
>
> After a pause, the team agreed. Mike, another team member, spoke up, "We learned that using total physical response with adolescents works." Again, the team agreed and the evidence confirmed.
>
> Vickie added, "It all boils down to fun. We learned that when you make the lesson fun, students are engaged." (personal communication, February 4, 2009)

The team sat pensively for a moment, then realized that future lessons need to be guided by past experience: (1) no future lessons will be developed unless they have an element of fun, (2) all future team lessons will include some total physical response component, and (3) checklists will be avoided as part of the instructional strategy. This team was thinking together to inform instruction and improve learning. Senge refers to this as "team learning" (1990, p. 244), an essential element of learning organizations.

Evaluation as Venture Capital for Ideas

The school improvement process is uniquely designed to generate ideas with potential to become a best practice, particularly when the ideas are fashioned into actionable hypotheses through the inquiry process. When educators take sufficient time to evaluate their school improvement in terms of effectiveness, impact, and student outcomes, a wealth of new ideas should emerge that have evidence supporting their value. Is that a common experience in school improvement today? Wouldn't it be wise to devote some time to determine why the best practice of evaluating our efforts is not a common practice?

Often, the improvement process identifies cause-and-effect relationships that can be refined, extended, and tested in other settings. These trends or patterns frequently point to a common need or a common strength. If a connection is revealed, such as the connection to extend protocols employed in biology to every subject area, schools are empowered to see new possibilities, generate new hypotheses, and improve student learning.

Final Thoughts

Evaluation in school improvement has been confused with collecting, aggregating, and reporting results rather than deep analysis. This chapter has described a comprehensive method to evaluate school improvement that is both formative in terms of improving procedures and practices, and summative in terms of making meaning of the results. Evaluation involves (1) comparing planned outcomes with actual outcomes to determine the reasons for any discrepancies, (2) identifying lessons learned to make sure schools and districts identify which school improvement practices make a difference, (3) applying lessons to future plans to improve the subsequent cycle, and (4) ensuring transparency by disseminating results to all stakeholders and inviting reflective analysis in the process. These simple aspects of the evaluation cycle help determine the degree to which hypotheses were realized and which targeted research-based strategies succeeded in closing learning gaps.

We challenge readers to view evaluation as part of the visioning process. This perspective gives teachers and administrators a "balcony view" of the process to ensure improvement practices have maximum impact and optimum sustainability. Evaluation is also a way of thinking, not just a process. School improvement can be described as an opportunity to capture the wealth of ideas and treat them as venture capital; evaluation helps identify and generate those ideas and to examine their impact on achievement. Chapter 7 will examine school improvement as a rich opportunity for leaders to distribute and increase leadership in learning.

Key Questions for Team Study

Evaluation is incomplete until lessons learned are recorded and next steps recommended.

How does this differ from the current practice in your organization?

Evaluation is the process of determining value.

To what degree does your current evaluation process determine the value of your efforts?

Evaluation is venture capital.

To what degree does your current evaluation process capture emerging ideas and strategies? What might you do to ensure that no good idea escapes without sufficient scrutiny?

7 ▶ Opportunity to Lead

The urgency of the hour calls for leaders of wise judgment and sound integrity—leaders not in love with money, but in love with justice; leaders not in love with publicity, but in love with humanity; leaders who can subject their particular egos to the greatness of the cause.

—*Martin Luther King Jr.*

MAY 30, 1:30 P.M. Byron was sitting in his office, proud of the fact that he had successfully graduated his twenty-second class from KCHS and that teachers, for the most part, were all checked out of school, engaged in a variety of summer activities. The days immediately following the close of school had provided Byron the unusual opportunity to reflect on what they had collectively accomplished and on what he personally had achieved. Byron's mind wandered to the issue of leadership and how far the profession had come since the days of valuing leaders who ran a tight ship. He thought about the leadership phases he had gone through—principal as an administrator and principal as instructional leader. This past year, more than any of the previous years, however, caused Byron to wonder if he was experiencing yet a third leadership phase, given the constant stream of fragmented demands on him and his time. For example, it seemed as though he was spending a considerable amount of time attending to the needs of individual staff members, particularly those who appeared to be left out. And, considering the growing demand for graduates who are prepared to meet the challenges of the twenty-first century, Byron realized that he must help the staff at KCHS think about old problems in new ways. More demands were also being placed on Byron's communication skills with teachers, students, and parents. More importantly, Byron felt as if he must personally model for his staff the kind of behavior they should be displaying in order to realize their vision of schooling. He was overcome with frustration and uncertainty about what next steps he should take to improve his leadership skills. He wondered if Yohannon might be able to shed some light on this issue during their breakfast meeting the next week.

Leadership for effective school improvement planning, as Byron discovered, is much different today than when the first improvement plans were created during the last century. Heightened public awareness of our foibles, improved technologies and ubiquitous communications, and a growing research basis combine to raise the expectations for success from the public and from us as a profession. As a result of these external and internal forces, policy makers are demanding that our educational institutions be led by "leaders who can subject their particular egos to the greatness of the cause," as Martin Luther King Jr. said in the epigraph (as cited in Carson, 2000, p. 177). We now know that a comprehensive needs analysis, informed application of best practices, and powerful monitoring have the capacity to yield continuous improvement in terms of process and to sustain gains in terms of student achievement results. Just as Martin Luther King Jr. advocated for the development of intelligent, courageous, and dedicated leaders to deal with the challenges of a new age, the field of education must also face the challenges of a new age with bold and committed leaders. This is one of the pressing needs of the hour. We begin by describing the challenges schools continue to face in these uncertain times.

The Leadership Famine

The Thomas B. Fordham Institute and the Broad Foundation (2003) report, "Our public education system confronts a leadership famine amidst a feast of 'certified' leaders" (p. 14). Upwards of "40 percent of [the United States'] 92,000 principals will become eligible to retire in the next four years" and "in many school systems, two-thirds of principals will reach retirement during this decade" (p. 39). Since that time, the leadership famine has become even more acute and will continue to grow for the foreseeable future.

In addition to scarcity of leadership, the principal's job is becoming more complex and more challenging as educational outcomes from schooling are coming under greater scrutiny (Leithwood & Riehl, 2003). Demographic shifts and economic changes not seen in decades continue to present new challenges for educational leaders. The Fordham and Broad report (2003) notes that "today's principals face a daunting situation. . . . Yet they have scant authority to make and execute important decisions . . ." (p. 17). To meet the demands of the contemporary education system, all aspects of school leadership, including teacher leadership, must be accessed and utilized. Even as these demands work at cross purposes with school improvement efforts, we contend that no other structure within public or private education holds as much promise as the school improvement process.

The Window of Opportunity

Schools are remarkably stable organizations, with clearly defined operating procedures—calendars, purchasing, budgeting, textbook adoptions—for almost everything. Such stability is also a common weakness, because regular structures are rarely used to manage large-scale improvements or changes (Beckhard & Harris, 1987). But while major changes are expensive in terms of districtwide communication requirements, time, and energy, school improvement is a unique and powerful opportunity just waiting to realize its potential. Evans (2001) notes that "innovations need information and frequent human contact to supply new facts and ideas, penetrate any confusion and uncertainty, and promote new forms of working together" (p. 138). Effective school improvement is collaborative; responsive to insights gleaned from comprehensive analysis of data; focused and limited to prioritized goals to reduce uncertainty; and designed to be implemented by working together across content, grade levels, or course sequences. We are adamant about the need for midcourse corrections because those adjustments are responsive to the context of teaching and learning at the local school level. School improvement is uniquely designed to accommodate innovations.

Just as schools are remarkably stable organizations, school improvement is well established within the overall structure of schools and school systems around the globe as the platform where opportunities for change are presented, debated, and initiated. The first generation of school improvement laid a foundation for the future by creating familiar structures, a common language, and improved data analysis. The challenge today is, "If you must have a plan, then learn from the schools that have done it well" (Reeves, 2009b, p. 43). Make sure that each cycle is an improvement over the previous, that best practices are established as common practice, and that creative best practices become the rule rather than the exception in schools everywhere. The following sections explain our optimism for the future.

A Contract-Neutral Process

School improvement is perhaps the area of greatest consensus in school systems today. While many debate priorities in curricular emphasis and the allocation of resources, few debate the importance of collaborative school improvement through a shared decision-making framework. Virtually every school system has negotiated a defined school improvement or shared decision-making policy that spells out explicitly the roles, responsibilities, and membership of school improvement teams. The process is by definition collaborative, and the process works best only when collaboration is real and extensive (Danielson, 2006).

Local school improvement teams often have greater discretion to select and implement innovations than the school board, as decisions about their function are already part of policy. Districts considering new expenditures or new programs are subject to a wide range of legal, procedural, and fiscal constraints that school-based improvement teams are not. School improvement teams have the opportunity and the obligation to do what is possible within the limits of time and resources by initiating sound changes to improve student learning. No other mechanism has been established for this purpose (to attempt something new and different), and as we have seen, school improvement is an institution not only in the United States, but also Australia, the United Kingdom, Canada, Singapore, and the Netherlands.

If issues arise that contradict the negotiated contract, improvement teams are again obligated to resolve those issues during the planning process. If, for some reason, an individual school inadvertently or even intentionally violates the teacher contract, there are procedures to remedy the situation. In practice, problems are usually resolved prior to the development or publication of the improvement plan, if for no other reason than appeal procedures have been defined for all. Because of the transparent, public nature of school improvement, its documents are part of the public record, and local policies precisely dictate how faculty members, parents, and students can access the details of the plan. Two examples illustrate this point.

Natrona County School District (2000) of Casper, Wyoming, adopted a policy in 1993 that described timelines, membership, access, purpose, and an appeals process if necessary. In Mukilteo, Washington, a similar policy not only publishes each plan, but also describes the parameters of school improvement and establishes an open and transparent calendar (Mukilteo School Board, 2006). These are hardly isolated examples, as the National School Board Association (NSBA) developed policy guidelines shortly after the No Child Left Behind Act was enacted in 2002. The NSBA policy recommends:

> School districts will support the improvement efforts of local schools by targeting district resources in a manner consistent with individual school priorities and needs, and by providing effective oversight to ensure that the improvement models and strategies selected by each failing school are appropriately aligned with state assessments in terms of the content knowledge and skills that are measured. (2002, p. 2)

School improvement has become such a fixture in school systems that it is full of opportunities to change professional practice through deep implementation. In an Illinois study, Weiss (2008) found that "shared decision making was consistent with improved student achievement and that teachers and principals both preferred a greater degree of collaboration around curriculum, instruction, and school-wide interventions" (pp. 130–139). Essentially, the collaborative nature of school improvement is designed to promote teacher leadership because of teachers' "significant influence on the performance of students [as well as on] the performance of other teachers and school leaders" (Reeves, 2008a, p. 2), their ability to identify champions, and their ability to differentiate roles in such a way that teachers are empowered and have the capacity to better meet students' academic and behavioral needs. School improvement is simply a win-win structure for schools.

A Collaborative Work Culture

Much has been written about the power of effective teamwork (Fullan, 2003; Fullan & Hargreaves, 1996; Garmston & Wellman, 1999; Schmoker, 2006). Judith Little (1990) found a strong relationship between defined aspects of collaboration and improvements in both teacher and student performance such as: (1) significant gains in achievement, (2) increased capability to establish and test hypotheses, (3) greater confidence among team members, (4) the ability of teachers to buttress others' strengths and assist in areas of weakness, (5) increased flexibility and resourcefulness, (6) improved decision-making skills, and (7) improved ability to support the needs of beginning teachers. School improvement for the next generation promotes each of these results through deep implementation, reflective inquiry, and distributed leadership. More than fifteen years have passed since Milbrey McLaughlin concluded that "the most promising strategy for sustained, substantive school improvement is developing the ability for school personnel to function as professional learning communities" (as cited in DuFour & Eaker, 1998, p. xi).

The evidence is compelling that collaborative teams produce better decisions than isolated experts (Hackman, 2002; Katzenbach & Smith, 1993; Surowiecki, 2004). Effective teams build shared commitment, collective skills, and task-appropriate coordination strategies, and they avoid the mutual antagonisms, trails of failure, and negative discussions that plague ineffective teams. Hackman (2002) identifies five conditions that increase the likelihood of effectiveness; these conditions exist when a team

1. Is a *real team* rather than a team in name only;
2. Has a *compelling direction* for its work;
3. Has an *enabling structure* that facilitates rather than impedes teamwork;
4. Operates within a *supportive organizational context*; and,
5. Has available ample *expert coaching* in teamwork. (p. 31)

The data teams (White, 2005a) of teachers at West Side Middle School in Elkhart Community Schools, Elkhart, Indiana, emulated Hackman's five conditions for effective teams. Effective teacher teamwork was the key to dramatic improvements in student vocabulary development at all grade levels. Teachers working in data teams assessed student content-area writing monthly, collectively scored the writing using a common rubric, and subsequently used what they learned from their analysis of the student data to determine next steps for their instruction. This monthly pattern of continuous improvement—action research—was punctuated with frequent meetings between Kristie Stutsman, the principal, and her data team leaders to determine collective progress toward their targeted school goal and how she could best support the efforts of classroom teachers.

Soft Accountability

School improvement also often allows leaders to use a soft approach to accountability, without the sanctions associated with hard accountability. Leaders can guide teams to display data; engage grade-level and department leaders; increase the level of transparency; and celebrate the granular, incremental gains that are predictive of larger long-term improvements and successes. In contrast, hard accountability exists when the stakes are high and risks perceived as severe. The best examples of hard accountability are state and federal policies, rules, and regulations that school districts and schools must adhere to in order to comply with their accountability expectations. This form of accountability includes typically serious consequences such as reconstitution of the school for multiple years of not making AYP under the state and federal accountability system.

Principals in Hawthorn, Illinois, implemented soft accountability structures by including routine requests for hypotheses to support faculty requests, appending probing questions to data displays, and scheduling routine updates from professional learning communities (PLCs) at monthly school faculty meetings. A particularly insightful approach is a requirement that each meeting close with a synthesis and description of next steps. Sweating the small stuff focuses our efforts to improve schools one process and one classroom at a time.

Soft accountability empowers teachers and principals to identify high-leverage improvement targets driven by small, well-focused actions; teams examine how well students perform by subgroup, chart and post the data, make meaning of the data by delineating related instructional and leadership practices, and then make improvements. We have found that effective day-by-day application of this soft accountability process increases the capacity of teachers and leaders to be effective players in the accountability arena by

> being proactive and open about school performance data, and by being able to hold their own in the contentious debate about the uses and misuses of achievement data in an era of high-stakes testing. (Fullan, 2001a, pp. 127–128)

Another example of soft accountability in action is illustrated by the work of Jean Creasbaum and her staff at Oslo Elementary School in Elkhart, Indiana. A walk through Oslo Elementary School, where student achievement results have improved steadily since the faculty instituted a number of soft accountability practices, reveals a clear focus on academic achievement and a pervasive interest in and use of data. Proudly displayed on the walls outside every classroom are artifacts of student writing and data, which depict the monthly improvement students have made. These data displays were not created in response to external pressure such as a central office mandate, but rather developed as an outgrowth of the staff's internal desire to improve their practice and thereby improve learning for their 654 students. The Oslo staff discovered that nothing makes them more accountable than having honest, hard, public conversations about their teaching and leadership practices and how they relate to student performance. Soft accountability, therefore, encourages participation through a transparent examination of data that is publicly displayed.

High Efficacy

Webster defines *efficacy* as "the power to produce an effect" (Gove, 1986, p. 725). Efficacy for the next generation of school improvement is knowing that one has the capacity to make a difference in the lives of others and acting on that knowledge to do so. Highly effective groups believe in their collective capacity to produce results and persevere through both internal and external difficulties to achieve those results. The RAND change-agent study (McLaughlin, 1990) found a staff's collective efficacy to be the most consistent variable related to school success.

Teachers with high efficacy expect students to work productively and believe students are mature enough to learn difficult concepts (Holliday, 2001). When students master these difficult concepts, teachers feel a part of the students' success. Teacher efficacy was also found to be a function of the quality of relationships they enjoy with their students (Reames & Spencer, 1998), as schools with high teacher efficacy tend to have similar policies for teachers; principals in these schools invite teachers to participate in decision making and focus on policies that make the school operate well.

Next-generation school improvement efforts facilitate both individual and group efficacy through the planning, implementation, monitoring, and evaluation cycle described in previous chapters. This cycle of continuous improvement not only leads to improved levels of student achievement, but also changes the way we view ourselves. Four steps critical to improving individual and group efficacy are: (1) limiting the number of SMART goals, (2) using clear goals as a daily guide, (3) engaging in meaning making as everyone's responsibility, and (4) recognizing the difference between compliance and commitment.

Limiting the Number of SMART Goals

Individual and group efficacy are negatively impacted by teacher and leader uncertainty. One of the greatest impediments to successful improvement efforts is the uncertainty that results when we lose focus by attempting to do more than we have the time or resources to realistically accomplish. For these reasons, next-generation school planners limit the number of goals to those that reflect only the school's highest priorities.

John Taylor—principal of Ben Davis Ninth Grade Center in Indianapolis, Indiana—and his staff realized the benefit of combining goals, which allowed them to reduce the number of goals from four to one (see chapter 3 on planning). Schools that reduce the number of goals appreciate the fact that even the most highly skilled group of people can only make so many decisions, learn and apply (well) only so many new skills, and sustain only so many initiatives before the feeling of being overwhelmed sets in and begins to erode both individual and group efficacy.

Using Clear Goals as a Daily Guide

Goals give the next-generation school improvement effort meaning. Goals drive us. Mike Schmoker (1999) comments that setting schoolwide academic goals has a powerful coalescing effect on teachers and leaders. He adds, "Goals themselves lead not only to success but also to the effectiveness and cohesion of a team" (p. 24). Moreover, Amabile and Kramer (2007) help us understand that a stronger sense of self-worth and self-efficacy results when people understand the goals of their organization and how they, as individuals, can contribute to the attainment of those goals. Next-generation school improvement goals translate schoolwide goals into specific classroom goals for teachers, thereby connecting school improvement to instruction. Moreover, teachers who help their students translate those aligned classroom goals into personalized student goals effectively bring into line all stakeholders in the improvement process.

Engaging in Meaning Making as Everyone's Responsibility

In a world where we can expect the pace of change to continue to increase exponentially and where everything influences everything else, we are learning that "individual efficacy influences group efficacy, and both influence a sense of identity for the individual practitioner and the group" (Garmston & Wellman, 1999, p. 163). Efficacy is a potent provocateur to these interactions because it is a determining factor in how people make meaning of data and resolve complex problems. For example, if individuals or groups feel little efficacy, then antitheses like blame, withdrawal, and lack of flexibility are likely to follow (Reeves, 2008a). But teachers and leaders with a healthy sense of self-efficacy are likely to expend more energy in their work, persevere longer, set more challenging goals, and continue in the face of failure. In other words, next-generation school improvement practitioners will avoid the problems of blame and inflexible thinking by asking challenging questions and conducting action research to test hypotheses and experiment with alternative strategies.

Recognizing the Difference Between Compliance and Commitment

Peter Senge (1990) contends that "there is a world of difference between compliance and commitment" (p. 221). Essentially, the difference between the two boils down to *accepting* something versus *wanting* something. That is, the committed person wants to attain a vision (for instance, to become a professional learning community) and because of that brings a certain energy and excitement to the task. Conversely, the compliant person accepts the vision, goes along with it, and may sincerely try to contribute, but doesn't bring the same level of vigor and passion. Pfeffer and Sutton (2006) note, "One of the most persistent and powerful social psychological processes is that of commitment—we are more likely to carry through on decisions we have made and are therefore committed to" (p. 199).

The next generation asks leaders and teachers working the school improvement process to make a significant shift in their use of pronouns—from a focus on "them" to a focus on "we," from a focus on the shortfalls of others and what "they" need to do to a focus on what "we" can do to continuously improve. That is, next-generation efforts will pursue collective commitments (DuFour et al., 2008) that can help practitioners concentrate their efforts on what they control and influence, which serves to strengthen and support their emotional health (Goleman, 1997) as well as their self-efficacy.

The Power of Distributed Leadership

We conclude this chapter the same way we started it—by talking about the critical importance of growing and sustaining what Fullan (2001b) refers to as "leadership appropriate for the times" (p. 135), which also echoes Martin Luther King Jr.'s epigraph comment that "in this period of transition and social change, there is a dire need for leaders who are calm and yet positive, leaders who avoid the extremes of 'hot-headedness' . . . who can subject their egos to the greatness of the cause" (as cited in Carson, 2000, p. 177). Fullan and King note that periods of transition and flux require a change in leadership. Fullan further suggested that in a culture of complexity, "our only hope is that many individuals working in concert can become as complex as the society they live in" (2001b, p. 136).

Call it what you will—"collaborative leadership" (Reeves, 2006, p. 51), a "coalition of leaders" (Fullan, 2005, p. 69), or "dispersed leadership" (DuFour et al., 2008, p. 331)—we have discovered that the work of school improvement for the next generation will be the collective work of many hands. In other words, the leadership is shared and dispersed among positional leaders within the district and the school, as well as with teachers who assume a strong lead in the soft accountability for student learning. When this happens, school improvement practitioners build the capacity of the organization to work together, plan together, and improve student learning together.

Teams are increasingly important to the next generation. Sosik and Dionne (1997) define teams as consisting of

> two or more individuals with complementary skills who interact with each other toward a common task-oriented purpose. Team members consider themselves to be collectively accountable for the attainment of goals. Teams are formed to serve organizational interests within departments, and across departments and divisions. (p. 449)

Next-generation school improvement teams have discovered that collective effort and brainpower is the most powerful force for improvement—teams tend to be "genuinely smarter than the smartest people within them" (Surowiecki, 2004, p. 182). Consequently, it is not uncommon to hear team members express appreciation for being able to share instructional strategies, talk about effective applications of nonfiction writing to better help students learn their content, or learn more powerful ways to increase reading comprehension with their students who struggle most. Next-generation school improvement practitioners have learned what Tom Peters (1987) discovered more than three decades ago, that "the best companies systematically [work] to liberate the previously underutilized energy and expertise of 'self-managing teams'" (p. 282).

Final Thoughts

School improvement offers almost unlimited opportunities to demonstrate leadership and to invite others to lead in various roles and with varying responsibilities. The process offers principals the opportunity to improve their school in every mundane action they take, and it offers faculty and staff the opportunity to implement practices and strategies that cultivate their own leadership abilities. Leadership has long been perceived to be important to effective functioning of the complex environment we call school. Leadership is also a scarce commodity, and the complexity and the challenges of leadership are too many and too large to achieve at the highest levels without assistance. Leaders who identify and cultivate shared leadership, nurture soft accountability, and engage in continuous improvement through collaboration will unleash the power of individual and collective teacher efficacy and build capacity that lasts.

Chapter 8 introduces the principle of "one thing" to school improvement. As we plan for the next generation, it is important that we stay focused, and do as Covey, Merrill, and Merrill (1994) suggest and make certain that "the main thing is to keep the main thing the main thing" (p. 75).

Key Questions for Team Study

Collective effort and intelligence are a powerful force for school improvement.
How do we build and sustain a culture of collaboration?

Soft accountability empowers leaders and teachers.
What is the process of soft accountability, and how does it work to empower school improvement practitioners?

Efficacy (self and group) is strongly related to improvements in learning.
Which components of the next-generation school improvement model are most closely related to building and sustaining highly efficacious individuals and groups?

School improvement is everyone's responsibility.
What are some of the reasons why it is it important to share or distribute leadership when it comes to school improvement efforts?

8 ▶ One Thing

Curly: "One thing. Just one thing.
You stick to that . . ."

Mitch: "That's great, but what's the one thing?"

Curly: "That's what you've gotta figure out."

—*Jack Palance as Curly, and Billy Crystal as Mitch in* City Slickers

JUNE 7, NOON. "Yohannon!" Byron waved as he carried the sack lunches through Civic Center Park. "My leadership team reminded me today how much we've stopped doing this year, but each of us has never been busier. What is that all about, Mr. Scientist?"

Yohannon laughed, then responded as Byron knew he would. "The work has always been complex, you just failed to give the small stuff the attention it deserved."

Byron responded, careful not to give away too much enthusiasm, "Well, we have cut back on announcements over the intercom, we dismiss meetings early if we aren't prepared or if we have achieved our objective, and teams are free not to do things they previously thought were obligations."

"Like what?" Yohannon asked.

"Marilyn came up with the idea that we begin to modify curricula on the basis of student need or faculty need rather than a fixed cycle. We have some folks who really have perfected their curricula to align with standards, especially visual arts and physical education. Our math department has long outpaced the state and competitor schools, so changes in curricula are now the prerogative of our departments, and teachers like it."

"Can you identify the one thing that has made the difference?"

After a long pause, Byron responded, "No, not yet."

As mentioned in the epigraph, Curly's secret to life was very simple, and his advice to find it was profound, with real implications for school improvement. Many first-generation improvement efforts attempt to implement the latest innovations, only to be frustrated when goals are not achieved. It is entirely possible to choose the right strategy to meet the needs identified through a quality planning process—and even design a master plan that is coordinated, cohesive, and connected—and still fall short of meeting one's goals. As KCHS discovered, deep implementation is difficult when faculty already have a very full agenda and when other priorities, traditions, and practices compete with otherwise appropriate SMART goals. Evans described it this way: "Though we exalt [change] in principle, we oppose it in practice" (2001, p. 25). This resistance stems not from open opposition so much as from underestimating the tasks we choose to implement. All too often we overpromise and underdeliver.

This brief chapter pursues the notion of Curly's one thing, offering examples from schools across the country where improvement teams creatively identified what they needed to do and did it. In this chapter, we will refer to the search for the one thing, the most important thing, as "Curly's Rule."

An Avalanche of Information

We have reviewed hundreds of school improvement plans that exceed 100 pages; the current school record for length stands at 256 pages, and the current district-level record at 259 goals and objectives. These monuments to overachievement are presumably to be completed in 180–200 days of instruction and professional development. We can weigh the likelihood of success for some school improvement plans merely by placing them on a bathroom scale. True, lengthy plans are just as apt to identify powerful instructional strategies as shorter plans, and often long, elaborate plans describe a deep understanding of best practices across content areas—but to little avail.

If your school improvement plan is a massive tome, your problem is the problem every reader faces every day: how to distill the avalanche of data that comes our way into meaningful, manageable chunks (Marzano, 2007). First-generation school improvement plans invariably are longer than they need to be, and teams struggle to summarize and focus their efforts. In our earlier discussion of the school improvement cycle, we stressed the crucial role of the inquiry process and of reflective analysis in the evaluation phase to help educators avoid those problems.

The data avalanche is compounded by extensive external reporting requirements that focus as much on fiscal controls and sign-offs as on improving achievement. If you work in a school system today, some bureaucratic requirements are unavoidable, and much progress has been made to consolidate applications, particularly from the U.S. Department of Education. A generation ago, it was not unusual for districts to submit separate federal program applications that were an inch thick, completely distinct from one another and, in some cases, in direct conflict with other program priorities and objectives. The documentarianism described in chapter 1 must end, and one remedy is to incorporate and integrate.

Incorporate and Integrate

To the degree that school improvement plan formats must conform to the governing agency template, schools that find ways to incorporate and integrate improvement sections will be well-served. One method is to incorporate all boilerplate language from each plan to delineate the difference between boilerplate text and the active improvement plan.

Incorporating and integrating school improvement sections is not always easy, as some states require separate professional development action plans to ensure that schools include thoughtful professional development rather than the "drive-by" trainings that once were common. An unintended consequence is that districts feel compelled to create two parallel improvement planning processes—one that addresses strategies to improve achievement, and one that addresses professional development to build capacity of teachers. This approach is less than optimum because a quality implementation plan will carefully attach needed professional development to the changes described in action steps and the strategies to be employed.

Lisa Lantrip of Wayne Township examined the statutory requirements for accountability planning in Indiana and found a creative way to incorporate and integrate critical components within a new template that reduced the length of the documents by half. She separated the boilerplate compliance elements from the substantive improvement elements. Many passages regarding compliance can be cut and pasted from year to year with only minor changes; this allows the improvement teams to both focus on drafting those passages that define what is important and work together to outline the smartest and most effective way to improve student achievement. Faculty and staff need to view the improvement plan as a change initiative blueprint that guides desired improvements in their own practice, and unless districts find a way to combine sections so that the documents are cohesive and clear, the avalanche of data will obscure the needed changes and communicate to all that much of the plan is already in place or that some sections are optional.

Focus on Improvement Only

Another way to pursue Curly's Rule is to insist that the plan address only improvements or changes in practice. If a school adopted a six-plus-one writing trait initiative five years ago, it need not describe that program again in the improvement plan. Many things become part of the school culture as unspoken expectations and need not be repeated. If the teacher handbook describes a nonnegotiable teaching cycle, it need not be included in the improvement plan. Next-generation improvement plans describe *only one thing*: how we will improve our practices to improve student achievement and meet the explicit SMART goal we developed. If teachers already meet routinely twice monthly in their PLC or data teams, there is no need for that to be included in the action plan. If, however, something different will be done during those meetings going forward, that change should be included in the improvement plan.

Readers may be asking, "Is it really that simple?" Yes, sort of. In most schools, many initiatives, like the writing initiative referenced earlier, have been introduced. They may have been implemented consistently, but they have not yet reached a degree of fidelity if best practices are not yet common across the school. In that case, schools should include language about what is being done in the writing initiative to sustain it and extend it. That, too, is an improvement. Curly's Rule works very nicely if practitioners hold themselves to the standard that only the items being improved will be included in the plan. After all, we want these improvements to eventually become part of our culture as unspoken expectations for excellence. An added benefit of addressing improvement only is it focuses thinking to provide evidence of exactly what we are doing, rather than casually assume we have "been there and done that."

The final benefit of an improvement-only approach is that the document (or substantive section of the document) serves as a "dashboard" for the entire school to reference. Short and focused plans are not unlike an NFL coach's game plan that the coach references as he monitors the game from the sidelines.

A district in Connecticut required every administrator and faculty member to carry their improvement plan at all times in their professional capacity for the entire academic year. If a principal's meeting is scheduled, the district said, bring the plan. If a district curriculum committee is meeting, bring the plan. Individual school plans should inform those meetings, and participants who see the benefits in one plan will not have to be directed to bring it back to their own team when they return to school. The expectation didn't cost much, but it communicated volumes: "What you're carrying is valuable and important, like a driver's license. Use it, learn from it, and glean ideas for it wherever your work takes you. Use it to redirect colleagues to our area of focus, and recommend changes to it when you learn something that could improve it." The cost was little, the potential benefit great. Curly would probably not carry a notebook, but he might be willing to carry a blueprint or map for improvement. School improvement leaders for the next generation should do just that.

Create a Common Focus

Many schools across North America continue to struggle with the school improvement process, finding it much easier to aggregate data—even rich data that describe antecedent practices by teachers and administrators—than to reduce their focus to one, two, or even three goals. When school leaders have the wisdom to adhere to Curly's Rule, that decision is almost always welcomed and accompanied with a sense of relief by those charged to implement the school improvement plan.

Hillhouse High School is one of two large urban high schools in New Haven, Connecticut. Lonnie Garris' career as principal has spanned the entire history of school improvement planning, and he wisely followed Curly's Rule in terms of establishing a common focus on school improvement efforts that would impact learning in every classroom every day.

After developing a schoolwide data team, Hillhouse discovered that many of the challenges students faced in career and technical education courses were also faced by students in social studies, science, fine arts, and English. After animated discussion and debate, the team selected a single intervention, Reading for Information (RFI), that would be applied to every department, every day. This goal aligns with Connecticut's Common Core of Learning, which represents the state's standard of an educated citizen in terms of skills, knowledge, and character expected of Connecticut's secondary school graduates and describes all teachers as teachers of literacy.

Hillhouse asked each department to select engaging articles that lent themselves to a common writing prompt consistent with the state assessment format, the Connecticut Academic Performance Test (CAPT), and a common presentation protocol. This allowed each department to work through its own curriculum in a way that increased proficiency in making connections, supporting conclusions with details from text, and recognizing relationships among concepts. PLC/data teams analyzed pretest data, identified gaps in student understanding, examined student work, and developed interventions to implement across the department. The goal was to improve the degree to which students read for information, as demonstrated by gains on the department assessments administered every three to four weeks as well as the CAPT. Whether enrolled in physical education or advanced calculus, students understood the protocol for RFI. The schoolwide focus helped students see the need to read for details, make connections, and support conclusions from text. An added benefit to the school was ready access to short-cycle data that pointed to emerging best practices and facilitated frequent midcourse corrections schoolwide. Curly would be proud.

Create a Common Structure

The Concord Community Schools Corporation of Indiana was one of the first school systems to negotiate into their teachers' contracts a districtwide provision that every teacher in every school would be afforded time to collaborate with their peers through routine, workday data team meetings at least twice a month. All staff expect to be supported in that endeavor with training and materials, and in exchange, to participate fully, gather and report related data, and share best practices across the corporation.

Wayne Stubbs, assistant superintendent of schools, notes,

> The data team process has communicated unequivocally that we value collaboration and we expect that collaboration to yield improved professional practices that increase achievement and close achievement gaps. The process serves as a reality check, as monitoring periodically reveals uneven implementation we need to address by differentiating support and resources. Teachers feel respected and they know data teams are here to stay. One other benefit: the single focus has prevented us from taking unproductive detours. (personal communication, February 24, 2009)

Many districts are applying Curly's Rule by determining what they want to become and working toward it.

Less Is More

Steve Achronovich, superintendent of schools in Greece, New York, applied Curly's Rule by simplifying the school improvement process in three ways. First, schools received training on SMART goals as the lever to improve capacity of faculty and increase student achievement at all levels. By establishing few concrete process goals, each school was given latitude to develop its own plan based on a comprehensive needs assessment of teaching practices, leadership actions, and student achievement. Second, schools were expected to self-assess their improvement plans and to be prepared to respond to questions such as, "How did you determine what to select and monitor to determine goal achievement?" Third, schools were given a set of guided questions to help them assess their current plan and develop their subsequent improvement based on a simplified understanding of what constitutes quality school improvement (see appendix B, pages 153–154).

While Greece enlisted some external assistance to generate the guided questions and to support school leadership teams, Achronovich's approach was designed to change the paradigm from compliance to thoughtful reflection and development of creative solutions. By using the guiding questions as their rubric, Achronovich released schools from the tyranny of central office forms.

Final Thoughts

School improvement needs to learn at least two things from Curly: (1) less really is more, because it requires us to rule out what we neither need nor want, take the time to determine what is really important, and accomplish those goals; and (2) this winnowing process must be figured out in collaboration. Teaching and learning are complex, and leadership is the process of making the complex as simple as possible. There is a reason why this chapter is short, and we think it would make Curly smile. Next, chapter 9 synthesizes our discussion by suggesting remedies to the pitfalls raised in chapter 2 and by reviewing the lessons learned by our principal at Kelly County High School.

Key Questions for Team Study

Schoolwide improvements are sustainable.
Why would schoolwide improvements have greater sustainability than changes made by a department, grade level, or individual?

Less is more.
What evidence would you accept at your school that this is true? Are you able to identify examples from your own experience?

Schools need to figure out their own "one thing."
How important is it for schools like Hillhouse, Greece Public Schools, and Concord to identify the solution that fits their situation?

Which of these school improvement innovations would be helpful in your community? Why?

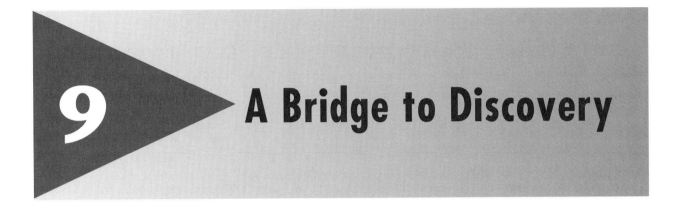

9 ▶ A Bridge to Discovery

f I have ever made any valuable discoveries, it has
been owing more to patient attention, than to any
other talent.

—Isaac Newton

JUNE 15, 7:10 A.M. "Byron, do you have a minute?" Without waiting for a response, Bill, the teacher association president, walked in and took a seat.

"Sure, Bill, what do you need?"

"Our department has been talking about last year's language arts goal based on those reports Kim has been generating."

It was Byron's turn to interrupt. "You mean the data Kim started tracking midyear?"

"Right, and get this. We had the right strategy, but I think we've discovered why we didn't get the results we wanted. Our plan was ahead of our ability to watch it unfold."

"So, our strategies were smart but how we pursued them was dumb, is that it?" Byron was impressed at how Bill could spin anything to shine a positive light on KCHS.

"That's pretty much it. We have all been asleep at the switch with this thing called school improvement. The way we have done it hasn't changed for a generation, and in the past, no matter how hard we tried, how skilled and committed we were, our design was a recipe for disaster because we ignored everything we know about teaching. Getting ready for this year, I am pumped, and Kim agrees we are finally on the right track. We got lucky last year with a smart strategy when we didn't have the data as evidence. All we have to do now is scaffold from simple to complex and easy to hard for each action step strategy to build capacity among the entire faculty and to improve student learning."

Byron's secretary leaned around the corner and said, "Your 7:15 appointment is here, Byron. I put them in your conference room."

"Thanks, Mary, and Bill, email that stuff, would you? Especially your take on scaffolding for kids and scaffolding for faculty as well. I'm intrigued. I'll look for your note, and thanks."

The school improvement process should engage teams of educators to discover solutions powerful enough to impact the status quo; it should go beyond past efforts to improve student learning and achievement. In chapters 1–8, we presented an array of strategies and tools to plan, implement, monitor, and evaluate school improvement. We provided a framework that has been applied to schools across North America and has shown the capacity to reveal trends and patterns, inform leadership and instruction, and generate insights that are unique to local schools and school systems. We believe school improvement offers educators a structure for growth and discovery with potential that has been largely untapped during the first generation of its widespread use. School improvement efforts have the potential to generate solutions that future research efforts can refine and validate. Such solutions can only emerge from the efforts to address chronically unmet student needs.

This chapter describes how each phase of the school improvement cycle adds value and capacity to the next phase. Throughout, we invite readers to learn from their colleagues and challenge readers to discover a new way of thinking about and responding to the tasks of school improvement.

A Cycle of Continuous Improvement for Success

Planning, implementation, monitoring, and evaluation are the building blocks of next-generation school improvement when they are supported with collaboration and accountability. The Leadership and Learning Center's PIM framework (Reeves, 2006) has been used to review almost three thousand improvement plans and has proven to be a useful tool in detecting strengths and weaknesses, revealing patterns and trends, and identifying leadership actions.

Our experience reviewing thousands of written plans against these criteria (see appendix A) and work supporting schools and district officials to identify the critical practices, approaches, and antecedent conditions necessary for the next generation of school improvement led to this book. To meet the changing needs of students, respond to new dynamics in terms of technology, and maintain a cohesive focus, schools will need the added clarity in focus and delivery that we have described in this resource.

Figure 9.1 illustrates the four critical components of the school improvement cycle with bulleted lists of the characteristics we have discussed that distinguish the extent of collaborative and accountable planning, implementation, monitoring, and evaluation necessary for the next generation of learners.

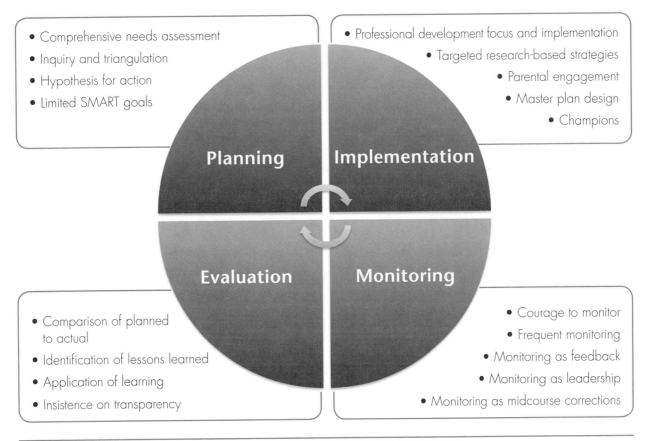

- Comprehensive needs assessment
- Inquiry and triangulation
- Hypothesis for action
- Limited SMART goals

- Professional development focus and implementation
- Targeted research-based strategies
- Parental engagement
- Master plan design
- Champions

Planning   **Implementation**

Evaluation   **Monitoring**

- Comparison of planned to actual
- Identification of lessons learned
- Application of learning
- Insistence on transparency

- Courage to monitor
- Frequent monitoring
- Monitoring as feedback
- Monitoring as leadership
- Monitoring as midcourse corrections

Figure 9.1: Process of school improvement for the next generation.

Planning

A comprehensive needs assessment lays the foundation for the next generation of school improvement efforts. It provides enough information about learning, teaching, and leading to ensure a thorough inquiry process that will yield insightful hypotheses for action. The inquiry process winnows the information by ruling out inconclusive data and ruling in meaningful cause-and-effect data. This ensures that the hypotheses generated address only the most pressing organizational needs with the smartest strategies. If the needs assessment is comprehensive and the inquiry process is reflective, hypotheses will produce a limited number of high-leverage, targeted, research-based strategies through each IF statement, and will guide development of SMART goals through each THEN response.

KCHS was beginning to demonstrate many of these leadership practices. We rejoin the principal and the teacher association president in Byron's office later that June morning.

Bill began again. "Oh yeah, almost forgot, the data part was really exciting. I was one of the few who did the strategy as designed and went deeper through the year. Fourteen percent of us, mostly English because we were really excited, showed 25–30 percent gains in the number of IEP kids who met standard. This happened even in my English 9 class. Folks who reported on the end-of-year survey that they didn't get it or needed training or more support basically saw flatline results for IEP kids.

"Kim's charts are pretty compelling: these skills are the weak link in terms of the HSPA, and that weakness is exacerbated for IEP and ELL subgroups. The walkthrough data are pretty revealing, too. Teachers who were observed addressing at least two of the four reciprocal teaching steps showed even higher gains than the rest of us, and the visual arts teachers actually had better gains than English teachers in April and May. The task now is to determine what the smartest idea with the greatest likelihood for success is. Just like Marilyn has been saying, we need to get clear on our hypothesis for action. Helen nailed it with the reading strategy, but not because of the data. We got lucky as a starting point last year."

The first-generation KCHS comprehensive needs assessment is compared to KCHS's next-generation comprehensive needs-assessment data in table 9.1. This table represents only a snapshot of the key findings and data analyzed, but it illustrates how the right data can go a long way to inform our thinking, creativity, and quality of decision making.

Table 9.1: KCHS First- Versus Next-Generation Comprehensive Needs

First-Generation School Improvement Plan	Next-Generation School Improvement Plan
Needs Assessment: Sixteen of thirty-two subgroups failed to make adequate yearly progress (AYP). In particular, students with individual education plans (IEPs), students eligible for free or reduced lunch (FRL), and African American boys did not meet standard.	Needs Assessment: Sixteen of thirty-two subgroups failed to make adequate yearly progress (AYP) and did not meet standard in the area of reading comprehension. In particular, students with individual education plans (IEPs) were 47 percent proficient; students eligible for free or reduced lunch (FRL) were 52 percent proficient; and African American boys were 58 percent proficient.

While Kelly County High School's initial needs assessment did prioritize three subgroups of students who did not make adequate yearly progress, it did not specify the content area or subskill in which improvement was needed, nor did the initial plan quantify its qualitative observations with hard data. What KCHS learned and then applied to their subsequent plan was that a comprehensive needs assessment must provide enough information to ensure a thorough process of discovery. When that occurs, the inquiry process is designed to yield insightful hypotheses for potential action.

Bill's conversation with Byron is reflected in the planning process depicted in table 9.2. This table compares the KCHS first-generation school improvement process of inquiry with a revised plan based upon inquiry process standards for the next generation.

Table 9.2: KCHS First- Versus Next-Generation Inquiry Process

First-Generation School Improvement Plan	Next-Generation School Improvement Plan
Causal Factors—What Didn't Work?	**Causal Factors—What Didn't Work?**
General education and special education teachers lacked structured teacher planning time. There was limited emphasis at all ability levels on higher-order thinking skills allowing students to apply strategies to comprehend, interpret, and evaluate informational text. Reading strategies were used inconsistently in all content areas. Proficiency tutorial programs lacked participation by IEP students.	Staff implemented the HSPA initiative unevenly (40 of 120 teachers implemented weekly, and only 10 implemented three times per week). The HSPA initiative was not monitored or measured often enough to determine professional development implementation needs (CWTs only occurred every other month, and data were not used). Some staff (30 of 120) developed formative assessments but there was not a collective schoolwide effort in this area.
Causal Factors—What Is Working?	**Causal Factors—What Is Working?**
Daily critical thinking activities aligned to each curriculum have been incorporated. Administrators and staff members in each department participate in a scheduled review of CWTs. Some teachers implement HSPA warm-up drills that incorporate revising and editing skills, open-ended response, and literary terms. Some teachers use the AP syllabus and AP required textbook to increase rigor in the classroom, administer timed writings every three weeks, and measure performance with the AP rubric.	Forty of 120 teachers implemented HSPA weekly and 10 implemented it three times per week, which seemed to produce increased results for some IEP students (gains from −11 percent to +34 percent) and African American students (gains from 2 percent to 29 percent). The more HSPA warm-up drills were used, the greater the gains were for IEP and African American students. Practice techniques are varied. Fifteen percent of KCHS faculty reported themselves as proficient on the staff survey or willing to teach others reading comprehension strategies.

Both Byron and Bill made a couple of discoveries about planning during their morning conversation. First, KCHS needed to do with planning what educators learned to do with standards in the early 1990s—either dramatically reduce them to what is absolutely essential or significantly increase the time to teach to them. Byron and Bill learned that the planning process must funnel information and prioritize data to generate a few essential hypotheses of action (goals and strategies to achieve them). Table 9.3 (page 136) provides KCHS hypotheses as the basis for developing precise goal and strategy statements.

They learned they were attempting to do too much in the time available. Critical to this process is the task of *ruling out* inconclusive and *ruling in* meaningful cause-and-effect data to ensure that the hypotheses address only the most pressing organizational needs with the smartest strategies. Second, Byron and Bill discovered how problematic decision making was when the KCHS staff dealt with opinion versus fact. Although KCHS staff collected anecdotal cause-and-effect data, they did not have hard data to support their assumptions—a problem that was corrected as they incorporated this learning into the next-generation plan for the following year. Once the essential hypotheses were generated, Bill and Byron redefined their goals to become SMART goals.

Table 9.3: KCHS Next-Generation IF/THEN Hypotheses

IF. . . (Action Step Strategies)	THEN. . . (SMART Goal Statements)
The KCHS improvement plan builds upon prior efforts by concentrating on a limited number of initiatives applied across the curriculum by all departments and teachers,	student achievement will increase for all students, as measured by improved attendance, grades, and scores in reading (comprehension) on the 2012 HSPA.
KCHS teachers consistently implement the HSPA warm-up drills (editing skills, open-ended response, and literary terms in lessons) at proficient or higher (based on rubric),	student achievement will increase, especially for IEP students and African American boys in reading (comprehension) on the 2012 HSPA.
KCHS teachers apply best practices in their classrooms in reading comprehension at proficient or higher (based on rubric),	student achievement will increase, especially for IEP students and African American boys who will score at proficient or higher on a common, monthly schoolwide assessment.

SMART goals are developed once school improvement teams have identified priority areas on which to focus their improvement efforts. SMART goals are created to build unity among the faculty, provide a clear direction, and set a standard of expectation against which school teams can determine whether improvement efforts are making a difference and to what degree. Table 9.4 depicts the first-generation KCHS goal statement compared to the SMART goal developed after applying next-generation improvement standards.

Table 9.4: KCHS First- Versus Next-Generation SMART Goal Development

First-Generation School Improvement Plan	Next-Generation School Improvement Plan
Goal 1: Students at KCHS will show increased achievement in reading on the spring 2012 HSPA. Specific improvement will be made by the IEP subgroup in all reading areas and performance strands (such as comprehension, literary analysis, and vocabulary).	Goal 1: KCHS will increase student (IEP subgroup and African American boys) achievement in reading (comprehension) on the 2012 HSPA from 47 percent to 63 percent for IEP students and 58 percent to 70 percent for African American boys by May of 2012.

Specific goals minimize interpretation and establish a common understanding of terms. *Measurable* goals ensure that a baseline is evident to focus efforts on the degree of growth anticipated and required. *Achievable* refers to whether the goal describes the closing of achievement gaps, *relevant* ensures that the goal is derived from the data analyzed in the comprehensive needs assessment, and *timely* ensures that each of the goals identifies specific dates for assessment and data collection/analysis. When hypotheses result from a quality inquiry process, goals will routinely be SMART and the strategies selected will be targeted and research based.

Implementation

JULY 10, 4:00 P.M. Byron was surprised that the leadership meeting ended early. He was also surprised at how well his leadership team responded to just a few changes in the process they would follow in the coming year. Byron smiled as he drove home, remembering the counsel of his young mentor: "If it doesn't become the most important work for your school leadership team, how will it become even remotely important for your entire faculty?" Byron began to recall how frequently Yohannon would pose questions as hypotheses, and he smiled again as the light changed. The template would change very little, the teams would not change at all, and the time available to complete the plan was as always, precious, limited, and in competition with a host of internal and community alternatives. The changes were relatively simple, and captured in these five parameters:

1. Action steps in the new plan were carefully delineated sequential protocols that directed faculty to change practice, and nothing could become an action step unless some change in professional practice could be measured in stages from introduction to mastery.

2. Strategies selected to meet the needs of students had to be targeted to the student groups whose performance warranted something better.

3. Timelines had to be specific (date or days of the week or month when monitoring would occur), sequential (progress from a lower level of implementation to a higher), and progressive—or back to the drawing board.

4. Professional development would no longer be like a smorgasbord from which you pick what you want, try it, and discard it; professional development would drive the changes in the plan, and every action step strategy would explicitly describe changes for kids and for adults requiring focused, embedded professional development.

5. Every component of the plan had to be mission critical, and every action step had to be sequential, progressive in terms of quality implementation, and rigorous in delivery and outcomes as the year unfolds; like its champion football team last season, KCHS would be better, faster, smarter, and stronger at the end of the season than at the beginning.

Byron hit the garage opener as he turned up the driveway, satisfied to be entering his twenty-third year at KCHS but determined to spend the next thirty minutes enjoying his backyard asters before checking his email.

The first-generation KCHS school improvement plan is contrasted in table 9.5 (page 138) to KCHS's next-generation master plan for implementation. Byron's parameters provided guidance in developing implementation strategies.

Table 9.5: KCHS First- Versus Next-Generation Master Plan Design

First-Generation School Improvement Plan				
Strategy/ Action Plan	**Formative/ Summative Measurement**	**Responsible Person**	**Resources Needed**	**Timeline**
Teachers will implement HSPA warm-up drills that incorporate revising and editing skills, open-ended response, and literary terms in lessons.	Benchmark test data Common assessments Classroom walkthroughs	Teachers English/language arts coordinator Department chairs	Released HSPA items Campus online HSPA Warm-Ups book: HPSA Coach Jumpstart HPSA Roadmap to HSPA	September 2011–February 2012
Next-Generation School Improvement Plan				
Strategy/ Action Plan	**Formative/ Summative Assessment**	**Responsible Person**	**Resources Needed**	**Timeline**
The percentage of teachers who implement the HSPA warm-up drills (editing skills, open-ended response, and literary terms in lessons) monthly at the "proficient" or higher levels, based on a locally developed rubric, will be increased.	The percentage of IEP and African American students scoring at the "proficient" or higher levels on monthly skill-based HSPA common formative assessments will be increased.	PLC/data team leaders with Kim as champion	Released HSPA items Campus online HSPA Warm-Ups book Scoring rubric with parent training three times a year HSPA common formative assessments Professional development in HSPA strategies	Baseline at standard 33 percent (see needs assessment) October 15: 45 percent of targeted students at standard January 15: 60 percent of targeted students at standard March 30: 75 percent of targeted students at standard

The implementation phase is the master plan realized; it carefully articulates the targeted strategies with a limited number of aligned, focused professional development initiatives. When these professional development initiatives are developed, quality of implementation and sustainability is ensured by addressing the needs of adult learners through embedded, proven, differentiated professional development. Parental engagement also needs to be woven into the fabric of a master plan in such a way as to ensure access, education, and transparent communication with parents at their convenience and in their native language whenever possible. Master plan design, as described in chapter 4, includes key attributes of progressive implementation; rigor; distributed leadership to champions of action steps; and precise, scheduled timelines for action. Table 9.6 provides a second example by contrasting the first generation attempt at master plan design at KCHS with a next-generation effort.

Table 9.6: KCHS First- Versus Next-Generation Master Plan Design

First-Generation School Improvement Plan				
Strategy/ Action Plan	**Formative/ Summative Measurement**	**Responsible Person**	**Resources Needed**	**Timeline**
Teachers will use the AP syllabus and AP textbook to increase rigor in the classroom.	Data from timed writings, rubrics, and free writes The AP rubric to measure performance	Pre-AP teachers and AP teachers	Released HSPA test HSPA coach Jumpstart HSPA Roadmap to HSPA AP rubric	Third week of grading cycle Timed writings every three weeks
Next-Generation School Improvement Plan				
Strategy/ Action Plan	**Formative/ Summative Assessment**	**Responsible Person**	**Resources Needed**	**Timeline**

All teachers will deliver lessons using AP syllabus format elements: (a) free-response questions, (b) practice using AP study skills/test-taking strategies, (c) topical outline, (d) daily agenda describing course topics, goals as student outcomes, and daily reflective activity.	1. The percentage of teachers self-reporting use of free-response questioning in at least one section
	2. The percentage of teachers self-reporting the syllabus format elements *a* through *d* (column 1) in at least one class section
	3. The percentage of CWT versus self-report observations
	4. The percentage of teachers self-reporting use of free-response questioning in at least three sections
	5. The percentage of teachers self-reporting the syllabus format elements *a* through *d* (column 1) in at least three sections
	6. Monthly monitoring of improved attendance by class section
	7. Year-to-year gains on AP enrollment and passing rates
		Marilyn to coordinate and display gains in terms of fidelity of implementation in foyer
		
		PLC leaders to gather formative data for Marilyn monthly
		
		Marilyn to monitor summative data
			Schoolwide professional development in AP protocols and syllabus format (all teachers and administrators):
			
			  Modeling and practice in free-response questions
			
			  AP study skills
			
			  Three daily agenda elements
			
			  Release time (substitutes) for one peer observation per staff member weekly from August to October and monthly from November to May
				September 15: All teachers/ principals receive professional development with modeling and guided practice in AP syllabus.
				
				October 30: Implement assessments 1–3 (column 2) with 100 percent fidelity in one class per teacher.
				
				March 31: Implement assessments 4–6 (column 2) with 100 percent fidelity in three classes per teacher.
				
				PLCs to report at monthly faculty meeting.

The first-generation effort was well intentioned to enlist all pre-AP and AP classrooms to adhere to the AP syllabus protocol, but the idea was neither supported with resources, clarified to establish a common language and understanding, nor resourced with sufficient professional development to build capacity across the faculty. This effort lacked the accountability that comes when specific individuals are tasked with the responsibility to coordinate implementation. Because the expectation was to begin full implementation immediately, the first-generation effort was unrealistic; the next-generation effort, however, included a progressive timeline that invited teachers to build capacity slowly, beginning in one classroom and extending to at least three. This plan is much more achievable for staff than an assumed fidelity of implementation for every teacher and every class. Quality implementation is a process of replacing assumptions about professional practice with guidance and support.

Monitoring and Evaluation

AUGUST 2, 2:30 P.M. "Slow down, Bill, you're going to lose me if you don't start connecting the dots," Byron said. "First, the idea to focus on higher-order thinking and to use the HSPA warm-ups to practice and strengthen revising, editing, and open-ended responses was a good one, but weren't we using growth to monitor how we were doing?" Byron was getting a little frustrated. "We used our walkthrough data and quarterly benchmarks, and departments had their own common assessments. If anything, we were getting back on that testing treadmill."

This time Bill slowed for emphasis. "The benchmarks tested more than revising and editing, right? Monitoring with that data just showed us people were complying, not improving."

"The problem wasn't the assessment, the problem was getting everyone to buy in and deliver the strategy," Byron agreed.

"Yes, and no. That is why we are so pumped about this. We needed to be more precisely aligned, just like that guaranteed viable curriculum stuff. We needed a short formative assessment that was constructed from simple to complex, easy to hard. But that's only half of the equation. Can I go on?"

Byron was struck by Bill's passion. "Don't let me get in your way, Bill, please."

"We need to monitor what we are doing in the same way. Last year we used only student tests to measure our implementation work. I don't know how I missed it, but when Kim and Karen and I met, it was suddenly so clear. Think about it, Byron, our strategy was for the whole faculty to get really good at teaching these key skills, but we didn't monitor or even consider where we were starting or where we were headed. We just knew that kids would do better on generic assessments and you guys would be happy during those classroom drive-bys you do every week." Bill sat down on the edge of his seat in anticipation of Byron's response.

"Classroom drive-bys, is that what you call the walkthroughs I busted myself to conduct every week?" Byron feigned indignation, and both men smiled.

"We would never teach kids that way," Bill said. "We'd never throw the work at them and let them sink or swim. I'd never plan to teach *Macbeth* and then give feedback on *Julius Caesar*, nor would I expect kids to get it all during the first month of school. Kim said it—we need to monitor and improve both student and teaching performance."

"You make too much sense, Bill. Pull together a small group from the school improvement team, include Kim as my representative, and I'll get a day of substitutes for all of you to develop the smartest monitoring and evaluation design you can. I want it good enough to use a decade from now, OK? Can you be ready by Thursday?"

As Bill knew, improvement plans pivot on effective monitoring strategies. Table 9.7 compares the first-generation KCHS school improvement plan with KCHS's application of next-generation strategies for monitoring.

Table 9.7: KCHS First- Versus Next-Generation Monitoring

First-Generation School Improvement Plan				
Strategy/ Action Plan	Formative/ Summative Measurement	Responsible Person	Resources Needed	Timeline
A reading initiative will be established in all departments.	Collect reading initiatives—all departments. Review lesson plans.	Teachers Department chairs	Sample district reading initiatives Teacher resources on higher levels of Bloom's Taxonomy	Department meetings each month August to December
Next-Generation School Improvement Plan				
Strategy/ Action Plan	Formative/ Summative Assessment	Responsible Person	Resources Needed	Timeline
The percentage of teachers who apply best practices monthly in reading comprehension at the "proficient" or higher levels, based on a locally developed rubric, will be increased.	The percent of IEP and African American students scoring at the "proficient" or higher levels on a common, monthly school-based reading comprehension assessment will be increased.	Content-area data team leaders	Professional development in reading comprehension Content-area reading comprehension support materials Scoring rubric with parent training three times per year Reading comprehension common assessment	Baseline October 15: 20 percent of targeted students at standard January 15: 45 percent of targeted students at standard March 15: 65 percent of targeted students at standard May 30: 90 percent of targeted students at standard

The monitoring phase frequently captures evidence of the degree to which the master plan is implemented with fidelity. It examines progress in student achievement, quality of adult implementation, and capacity building. Selection of insightful information sentinels that indicate early warning or early success are also critical to monitoring, as compliance activities rarely inform meaningful midcourse adjustments.

Monitoring frequency refers to the timeliness of feedback received, particularly corrective feedback that identifies strengths and challenges participants to stretch to a higher level of rigor and a more consistent delivery of instructional and leadership practices.

The evaluation plan allows the school to compare planned outcomes with achieved outcomes. Table 9.8 compares the first generation of the KCHS school improvement evaluation to its latest iteration following efforts to meet next-generation improvement standards.

Table 9.8: KCHS First- Versus Next-Generation Evaluation Cycle

First-Generation School Improvement Plan				
Strategy/ Action Plan	**Formative/ Summative Measurement**	**Responsible Person**	**Resources Needed**	**Timeline**
Monitoring and evaluation will occur.	KCHS interim fall/ spring English/ language arts assessments; English department common assessments; HSPA spring results	English department; Learning improvement team; Principals		Quarterly October January March May
Next-Generation School Improvement Plan				
Evaluation Cycle: At the end of the 2011–2012 school year, KCHS will collectively engage in a process to compare planned outcomes with achieved outcomes, how compared results (positive and negative) are communicated to primary stakeholders (families, educators, staff, patrons, partners, and the public), and how lessons learned will be applied to future (2012–2013 school year) school improvement planning.				

The final component of this phase is evaluation, a process described in chapter 6 as both formative and summative. It provides key input for the next cycle of improvement by informing the comprehensive needs assessment with lessons learned and recommending next steps. The evaluation process is simple in itself, but as part of a powerful cycle of continuous improvement, evaluation has real potential to improve schools and build a culture of evidence. As the data shown in earlier chapters suggest, schools that implement these practices well are more apt to reach higher achievement gains than schools that implement casually. Evaluation is neither a one-time event, nor a mere reporting of results, but rather a profound form of organizational and team learning.

Final Thoughts

In this final chapter, we reviewed the phases of the next-generation school improvement process. We illustrated how each phase is connected to the others and emphasized the need to apply our best thinking at every juncture to plan the most effective strategies. The key to success is to make sure strategies are then implemented deeply, monitored with agility and precision, and evaluated with insight.

Our research and experience have shown us that there is a strong relationship between completing the planning, implementation, monitoring, and evaluation phases at a high level and improved achievement. When teams sweat the small stuff, they discover that deep implementation that results in even one best practice becoming common practice affects conversation as well as competence, and efficacy as well as performance.

We are convinced that the collective wisdom of school teams is more than capable of improving schools by improving professional practice, which in turn improves achievement. We are equally convinced that educators can and should learn lessons each year that allow them to get off the rollercoaster of student achievement and pursue a path of steady growth. Each phase—planning, implementation, monitoring, and evaluation—needs to be treated as an opportunity for discovery. Leaders, especially, must insist on clarity and explicit descriptions of protocols to replace the casualness and presumption that have characterized the first generation of school improvement.

School improvement need not be tedious or overwhelming. Efforts to simplify and apply Curly's Rule will go a long way toward improving instruction and improving achievement. Schools that realistically assess the level of complexity will select only the most important and effective strategies and interventions. They will not only increase the level of collective efficacy but will get better over time and more responsive to the needs of students in their care.

The characters from KCHS are not entirely fictional. Their ability to change course and pursue the skills and attributes of leadership in school improvement in order to serve a next generation represents the same attitudes, insight, and intelligence we encounter from educators every day.

Curly taught us to change one thing well. Our hope is that from this volume, you will capture the moment, seize the day, and use the school improvement structure to make real and lasting improvements in this most complex business we call school.

Appendix A

The Leadership and Learning Center's Planning, Implementation, and Monitoring Framework

The following depicts a partial three-point rubric used by the authors to assess school improvement efforts since 2004 (Leadership and Learning Center, 2005b). For this example, only one sample item is included for each of the PIM framework elements; certified reviewers administer the entire assessment to reveal correlations between these school improvement practices and student achievement. Sample items distinguish between traditional practices and next-generation practices. For a school improvement element to be assessed as proficient, all criteria need to be evident. To be assessed as exemplary, reviewers determine that schools can demonstrate all the criteria required in proficient plus those required in exemplary. The authors created the framework, and subsequent work with clients revealed the need for a comprehensive look at school improvement for the next generation provided by this resource.

Planning		
Comprehensive Needs Assessment		
Exemplary	**Proficient**	**Needs Improvement**
Challenges are specified in student achievement, teaching, and leadership practices.	Challenges in both student achievement and adult practices (areas in need of improvement) are specific enough to guide and facilitate other components of this school improvement plan.	Challenges are limited to student achievement or adult practices, but not both; it is difficult to determine what needs to change at the school, based on data presented.
Inquiry Process		
The process yields prioritized hypotheses for action that informs *all* goal statements and action plan strategies.	The process yields at least one hypothesis for action that informs goal statements and action plan strategies.	Plan has at least six areas of action and fails to develop a single hypothesis to narrow priorities for action.

continued ➡

SMART Goals		
Specific Statements		
All school improvement goals are specific to standards (content areas) and subskills within the standard.	One or more school improvement goals are specific in terms of content (related to content-area standard and subskills within that content area).	School improvement goals tend to address general content areas, but do not address standards and related subskills.
Measurable Statements		
The school improvement plan establishes clear baseline data for *all* of its goals.	The majority of school improvement goals identify baseline data to measure progress toward achieving the goals.	Less than 50 percent of school improvement goals identify the baseline data needed to measure progress toward goal attainment.
Achievable Statements		
All goals are sufficiently challenging to close learning gaps in three to five years for targeted subgroups or subskills.	The majority of school improvement goals are sufficiently challenging to close learning gaps in three to five years for targeted subgroups or subskills, (for instance, percentage gains are significant enough to eliminate the achievement gap in three to five years).	Less than 50 percent of school improvement goals are sufficiently challenging. As a result, achieving them will make little difference to the school's overall level of student achievement and will not close achievement gaps.
Criteria for Determining Whether Goal Is Achievable: Minimal Growth in Student Achievement Quartiles From Baseline to Close Gaps: 20 percent growth in the first quartile, 12 percent growth in the second quartile, 7 percent growth in the third quartile, and 4 percent growth in the highest quartile.		
Relevant Statements		
All goals represent urgent, critical needs within the school and align with priorities established through the inquiry process.	The majority of school improvement goals align with priorities established through the inquiry process.	Less than 50 percent of school improvement goals align with priorities established through the inquiry process.
Timely Statements		
All of the school improvement goals identify specific dates (season, month, date) for assessment, data collection, and analysis.	The majority of school improvement goals identify specific dates (season, month, date) for assessment.	Less than 50 percent of school improvement goals identify a specific window (season, month, date) of time for assessment.

Implementation

Targeted Research-Based Strategies

Exemplary	Proficient	Needs Improvement
All schoolwide programs or strategies (NCLB research-based programs, collaborative scoring, dual block algebra, looping, tailored summer school) specify the student subgroup that needs the service.	A majority of schoolwide programs or strategies (NCLB research-based programs, collaborative scoring, dual block algebra, looping, tailored summer school) specify the student subgroup that needs the service.	Less than 50 percent of schoolwide programs or strategies specified are informed by the research from effective classroom and school practices, or less than 50 percent of schoolwide programs or strategies specify the student subgroup that needs the service.

Master Plan Design

All of the action steps and timelines for each objective and strategy are coordinated with each other.	A majority of the action steps and timelines for each objective and strategy are coordinated with each other.	Less than 50 percent of the action steps and timelines for each objective and strategy are coordinated with each other.

Professional Development Focus

The professional development focus is limited to less than three professional development initiatives that are well aligned with school and district goals to impact student achievement.	The professional development focus includes less than five professional development initiatives that are well aligned with school and district goals to impact student achievement.	The professional development plan lacks focus; plans tend to be too extensive with multiple and/or unrelated professional development strategies.

Professional Development Implementation

Professional development support is provided for *all* key initiatives in multiple ways. Clear evidence exists that coaching/mentoring is planned schoolwide (coaching, mentoring cadres, peer observations, lesson study).	Professional development support (time, patient and persistent coaching, mentoring is linked with initiatives, multiple opportunities for training, or retraining are provided to support teachers and build capacity) is evident.	Professional development support is not identified or is not specifically linked to key initiatives described in action steps. Coaching/mentoring is incidental to the school improvement plan.

Parental Engagement

Action steps for *all* goal areas describe parental training and education to enhance involvement in their student's academic achievement.	Action steps, within at least one goal area, describe parental training and education to enhance involvement in their student's academic achievement.	Actions steps do not describe parental training and education.

continued ➡

Monitoring and Evaluation

Monitoring Plan

Exemplary	Proficient	Needs Improvement
Student achievement assessment data monitoring includes a range of assessment data (annual assessments, quarterly benchmarks, monthly probes, and common formative assessments) evident in each goal area.	Student achievement assessment data monitoring includes a range of assessment data (annual assessments, quarterly benchmarks, monthly probes, common formative assessments) evident throughout the school improvement plan.	Student achievement assessment data monitoring is limited to annual student achievement results.

Monitoring Frequency

Monitoring schedules are described that review student performance, teaching practices, and leadership practices.	Monitoring schedules exist to review both student performance and some teaching practices.	Monitoring schedules may exist to review student achievement or teaching practices, but not both.

Evaluation

The evaluation plan is designed explicitly to describe the steps that the school needs to take to institutionalize successes and eliminate unsuccessful practices.	The evaluation plan is designed to be transparent in describing how compared results (positive and negative) are communicated to primary stakeholders (families, educators, staff, patrons, partners, and the public).	The evaluation plan is not designed to describe the process for communicating results.

Leadership and Learning Center, 2005b, used with permission

Hillsboro, Oregon, School Improvement Evaluation Template 2007–2010

The Hillsboro, Oregon, school district developed the following evaluation template to ensure reflective analysis of the school improvement plan itself, beginning by comparing goal statements with actual achievement outcomes (Leadership and Learning Center, 2005a). If planned goals were not achieved, comparing actual goals to planned goals provides insight into flaws of the current plan. If goals were exceeded dramatically, the comparison helps teams determine why they underestimated student performance. The second level of evaluation pertains to lessons learned and how schools will apply that learning. Hillsboro also uses a three-tier accountability system based on Reeves' *Accountability in Action* (2004b).

Evaluation: Compare planned against achieved outcomes (Summarize impressions, recall supporting information, compare, contrast, analyze, infer, and determine cause-and-effect relationships.) This section applies to the entire plan.	
We Planned These . . . (Goals, Tier II Indicators, Results Indicators)	**We Achieved These . . .** (Goals, Tier II Indicators, Results Indicators)
Applying: (Construct new learnings and applications.)	
We Learned . . .	**We Will Apply These Learnings to Next Year's School Improvement Plan . . .**
School Narrative: Tier III (Explain the relationship between Tier I and Tier II.)	

Montgomery, 2009, used with permission

Hawthorn, Illinois, School Improvement Evaluation Template 2009

Hawthorn, Illinois, chose to go one step deeper in terms of evaluation by describing a series of anticipated changes for students, staff, and parents. Both the Hillsboro template and the Hawthorn template represent emerging best practices in districts that are committed to making sure school improvement is evaluated in such a way as to reveal lessons learned that will then inform next steps.

Evaluation Cycle: (Compare planned against achieved outcomes.)	
Evaluation (Analysis): (Summarize impressions, recall supporting information, compare, contrast, analyze, infer, and determine cause-and-effect relationships.)	
We Planned These . . . (Goals, Tier II Indicators, Results Indicators)	**We Achieved These . . .** (Goals, Results Indicators)
Application: (Construct new learnings and applications.)	
We Learned . . .	**We Will Apply These Learnings to Next Year's SIP . . .**

What new knowledge, skills, and attitudes toward learning will result from this improvement cycle (action research)? What will it look like for students, staff, and parents?		
Students	**Staff**	**Parents**

Zook, Oker, & Cerauli, 2008, used with permission

Innovations Configuration Map for Five-Step Data Team Process

A configuration map is a means of describing what an innovation (such as data teams) looks like when fully implemented (Hall & Hord, 2006). The following configuration map describes the behaviors and practices of data teams in Elkhart Public Schools as they move from the "Not Proficient" status toward the "Exemplary" status. By doing so, the teams increasingly approach the more ideal practices pursued in the school district.

A configuration map is divided into the operational characteristics or key components of the innovation which distinguish it from other approaches. For each component in this data team map there are four stages in the implementation process ranging from "Exemplary" (the desired state) to "Not Proficient" (implementation has not yet begun). This framework differs from many rubrics in that the operational characteristics are holistic rather than analytical.

Component Description: Teachers collectively examine how well students are doing, relate this to how they are teaching, and then make midcourse corrections to help all students achieve high standards.

$\longleftarrow \hspace{6cm} \longrightarrow$

Exemplary	Proficient	Progressing	Not Proficient
(4)	(3)	(2)	(1)
All criteria for the proficient category have been successfully met. In addition: Data team members provide support (coaching and modeling) and guidance to other data teams who might be struggling with parts of the process.	Teachers apply the data team process smoothly with minimal management problems. Teachers routinely examine data from common formative assessments to analyze strengths/obstacles to "proficient and higher" student work. Teachers establish goals directly related to annual school goals. Teachers select one to two common instructional strategies to improve current levels of achievement. Teachers agree on what proficient use of the instructional strategies looks like.	Teachers manage the data team process with varying degrees of efficiency. The flow of actions is often disjointed, uneven, and uncertain. Staff members participate in the data team process. Findings generated by this process are beginning to influence classroom practices. Teachers may misinterpret the intent of selecting instructional strategy; they tend to select many instructional strategies they might use during teaching without reaching agreement as to what fidelity of use of the strategies actually looks like.	Teachers take no discernible action toward learning about or using the data team concept. Some staff members participate in pilot action projects. The sharing of findings is largely informal. Teachers demonstrate little attachment to anything or anybody, therefore teacher isolation predominates. Teachers seem more concerned with their own identity than a sense of shared community.

continued ➡

Exemplary	Proficient	Progressing	Not Proficient
(4)	(3)	(2)	(1)
Teachers explore and experiment with alternative combinations of data team practices (for example, meet twice a month to examine together how well students are doing, relate this to how they are teaching, and then make improvements) to maximize student outcomes. Teachers identify desired results from both the student as well as the adult practices.	Teachers describe desired student result indicators. Teachers assess efforts and reflect on teaching to determine next steps.	Teachers may or may not spend time reflecting on the process prior to moving on.	Teachers either never or rarely take time to share ideas and best lessons with their colleagues to develop and improve instruction.

Hall & Hord, 2006, used with permission

Appendix B

Guided Questions for School Improvement for the Next Generation

Guiding Questions
Planning and Inquiry
How do you set up your planning process and calendar to ensure systematic data analysis? In what ways have you addressed the issue of competing priorities throughout the fiscal year?
What trigger mechanisms are in place to ensure disaggregated data identifies students most in need?
How does your planning process provide for midcourse corrections and adjustments on the basis of the data being monitored (learning, teaching, or leadership)?
What are the staffing issues associated with needs projection? What human resources are committed to this effort, and how is information used by leadership and the community?
How does needs projection interface with your decision-making process? Do you use a specific model to identify such needs? Is there a bridge to other information systems?
Within your management system, what process exists for identifying trends?
Blueprint for Implementation
How would you describe your use of planned midcourse corrections and adjustments on the basis of the data being monitored (learning, teaching, or leadership)?
Describe the process you use to access and respond to data in your management system?
To what degree are action steps supported by professional development?
How would you describe the process for distributing leadership/responsibilities?

continued ➡

Guiding Questions
Monitoring and Evaluation
How would you describe the monitoring process that allows you to use your planned midcourse corrections and adjustments in targeted areas (learning, teaching, or leadership)? How would you describe the benefits of a systems approach to planning, implementation, monitoring, and evaluation that you have selected? How has your approach improved decision making? What barriers have you encountered in this process? What learning has occurred for you that will affect future planning, implementation, and monitoring efforts? What is needed over the long term to ensure that your system is fully functioning and self-sustaining? Please address both technical issues and any relevant cultural, structural, or personnel issues.

References and Resources

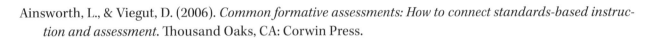

Ainsworth, L., & Viegut, D. (2006). *Common formative assessments: How to connect standards-based instruction and assessment.* Thousand Oaks, CA: Corwin Press.

Allen, L., & Glickman, C. D. (1992, March). School improvement: The elusive faces of shared governance. *NASSP Bulletin, 76*(542), 80–87.

Amabile, T. M., & Kramer, S. J. (2007, May). Inner work life: Understanding the subtext of business performance. *Harvard Business Review, 85*(5), 72–83.

Anderson, B. L. (1993, September). The stages of systemic change. *Educational Leadership, 51*(1), 14–17.

Anderson, L. W., & Krathwohl, D. R. (Eds.). (2001). *A taxonomy for learning, teaching, and assessing: A revision of Bloom's Taxonomy of educational objectives.* New York: Longman.

Anderson, T. J. (2004). Integrating decentralized strategy making and strategic planning processes in dynamic environments. *Journal of Management Studies, 41,* 1271–1299.

Antunez, B. (2002). *English language learners and the five essential components of reading instruction.* Accessed at www.readingrockets.org/article/341 on September 6, 2007.

Arens, A. B., Loman, K. L., Cunningham, P. M., & Hall, D. P. (2005). *The teacher's guide to big blocks: A multi-method, multilevel framework.* Greensboro, NC: Carson-Dellosa.

Armstrong, J. S. (1982, July/September). The value of formal planning for strategic decisions: Review of empirical research. *Strategic Management Journal, 3,* 197–211.

Banathy, B. H. (1996). *Designing social systems in a changing world.* New York: Plenum Press.

Barton, P. E., & Coley, R. J. (2008, December/2009, January). Measuring the achievement elephant. *Educational Leadership, 66*(4), 30–33.

Basham, V., & Lunenburg, F. C. (1989, March). *Strategic planning, student achievement and school district financial and demographic factors.* Paper presented at the Annual Meeting of the American Educational Research Association, San Francisco.

Bauer, S. C. (1992, July). Myth, consensus, and change. *Executive Educator, 14*(7), 26–28.

Beach, R. H., & Lindahl, R. A. (2007). The role of planning in the school improvement process. *Educational Planning, 16*(2), 19–43.

Beckhard, R., & Harris, R. T. (1987). *Organizational transitions: managing complex change.* Boston: Addison-Wesley.

Beckhard, R., & Pritchard, W. (1992). *Changing the essence: The art of creating and leading fundamental change in organizations.* San Francisco: Jossey-Bass.

Bell, T. H. (1974). *A performance accountability system for school administrators.* West Nyack, NY: Parker.

Bergeson, T., & Heuschel, M. A. (2005). *School improvement planning process guide.* Olympia, WA: Office of Superintendent of Public Instruction. Accessed at www.k12.wa.us/SchoolImprovement/pubdocs/SIPGuide.pdf on July 15, 2008.

Berliner, D. (1994). Expertise: The wonders of exemplary performance. In J. N. Mangieri & C. Collins Block (Eds.), *Creating powerful thinking in teachers and students* (pp. 141–186). Fort Worth, TX: Holt, Rinehart and Winston.

Bernhardt, V. L. (1999). *The school portfolio: A comprehensive framework for school improvement* (2nd ed.). Larchmont, NY: Eye On Education.

Bernhardt, V. L. (2004). *Data analysis for continuous school improvement* (2nd ed.). Larchmont, NY: Eye On Education.

Birman, B. F., Reeve, A. L., & Sattler, C. L. (1998). *The Eisenhower professional development program: Emerging themes from six districts.* Washington, DC: U.S. Department of Education.

Boyatzis, R., & McKee, A. (2005). *Resonant leadership.* Boston: Harvard Business School Press.

Bradberry, T., & Greaves, J. (2003). *The emotional intelligence quickbook: Everything you need to know.* San Diego, CA: TalentSmart.

Bradley, A. (1993, July 14). "Strong democracy" yields improvement in Chicago reforms. *Education Week, 12*(39), 1–13.

Bransford, J. D., Brown, A. L., & Cocking, R. R. (Eds.). (2000). *How people learn: Brain, mind, experience, and school.* Washington, DC: National Academy Press.

Brookover, W. B., & Lezotte, L. W. (1979). *Changes in school characteristics coincident with changes in student achievement* (Occasional Paper No. 17). East Lansing: Michigan State University Institute for Research on Teaching. (ERIC Document Reproduction Service No. ED181005)

Brophy, J. E. (1979). *Teacher behavior and its effects* (Occasional Paper No. 25). East Lansing: Michigan State University Institute for Research on Teaching. (ERIC Document Reproduction Service No. ED181014)

Bryk, A. S., Sebring, P. B., Kerbow, D., Rollow, S., & Easton, J. Q. (1998). *Charting Chicago school reform: Democratic localism as a lever for change.* Boulder, CO: Westview Press.

Bryson, J. M., & Roering, W. D. (1987). Applying private-sector strategic planning in the public sector. *Journal of the American Planning Association, 53,* 9–22.

Buchanan, J., & Khamis, M. (1999). Teacher renewal, peer observations and the pursuit of best practice. *Issues in Educational Research, 9*(1), 1–14.

Burns, J. M. (1978). *Leadership.* New York: Harper & Row.

Calhoun, E. F. (2002, March). Action research for school improvement. *Educational Leadership, 59*(6), 18–23.

Carson, C. (Ed.). (2000). *The papers of Martin Luther King, Jr. (Vol. 4): Symbol of the movement, January 1957–December 1958.* Berkeley: University of California Press.

Casciaro, T., & Lobo, M. S. (2005, June). Competent jerks, lovable fools, and the formation of social networks. *Harvard Business Review, 83*(6), 92–99.

Cepela, G. D. (2008). School improvement planning in two urban middle schools. *Dissertation Abstracts International, 68,* 4554. (UMI No. 3290553)

Clark County School District. (2009, April). *School improvement rubric.* Las Vegas, NV: Author.

Colvin, G. (2008). *Talent is overrated: What really separates world-class performers from everybody else.* New York: Penguin.

Connecticut State Board of Education. (2004). *Position statement on science education.* Accessed at www.sde.ct.gov/sde/LIB/sde/pdf/board/Position_Statement_Science_Ed.pdf on January 13, 2006.

Cotton, K. (2003). *Principals and student achievement: What the research says.* Alexandria, VA: Association for Supervision and Curriculum Development.

Covey, S. (1989). *The seven habits of highly effective people.* New York: Simon & Schuster.

Covey, S., Merrill, R. A., & Merrill, R. R. (1994). *First things first.* New York: Simon & Schuster.

Culham, R. (2003). *6+1 traits of writing: The complete guide, grades 3 and up.* New York: Scholastic Professional Books.

Danielson, C. (2006). *Teacher leadership that strengthens professional practice.* Alexandria, VA: Association for Supervision and Curriculum Development.

Danielson, C., & McGreal, T. L. (2000). *Teaching evaluation to enhance professional practice.* Alexandria, VA: Association for Supervision and Curriculum Development.

Darling-Hammond, L. (1997). *The right to learn: A blueprint for creating schools that work.* San Francisco: Jossey-Bass.

Deutschman, A. (2007). *Change or die: The three keys to change at work and in life.* New York: HarperCollins.

Doud, J. L. (1995, Spring). Planning for school improvement: A curriculum model for school based evaluation. *Peabody Journal of Education, 70,* 175–187.

DuFour, R., DuFour, R., & Eaker, R. (2006). *Professional learning communities at work plan book.* Bloomington, IN: Solution Tree Press.

DuFour, R., DuFour, R., & Eaker, R. (2008). *Revisiting professional learning communities at work: New insights for improving schools.* Bloomington, IN: Solution Tree Press.

DuFour, R., & Eaker, R. (1998). *Professional learning communities at work: Best practices for enhancing student achievement.* Bloomington, IN: Solution Tree Press.

DuFour, R., Eaker, R., & DuFour, R. (Eds.). (2005). *On common ground: The power of professional learning communities.* Bloomington, IN: Solution Tree Press.

Echevarria, J., Vogt, M., & Short, D. (2004). *Making content comprehensible for English learners: The SIOP model* (2nd ed.). Needham Heights, MA: Allyn & Bacon.

Edmonds, R. R. (1979). Effective schools for the urban poor. *Educational Leadership, 37*(1), 15–18, 20–24.

Eide, P. A. (2001, January). Coping with change: Educational reform in literacy practice. *Primary Voices, 9*(3), 15–20.

Elmore, R. (1996, Spring). Getting to scale with good educational practice. *Harvard Educational Review, 66*(1), 1–26.

Elmore, R. (2000, Winter). *Building a new structure for school leadership.* Washington, DC: Albert Shanker Institute.

Elmore, R. (2002, January/February). The limits of change. *Harvard Education Letter.* Accessed at www .edletter.org/past/issues/2002-jf/limitsofchange.shtml on July 28, 2009.

Elmore, R. F. (2004). *Knowing the right thing to do: School improvement and performance-based accountability.* Washington, DC: NGA Center for Best Practices.

Elmore, R. (2007). *School reform from the inside out: Policy, practice, and performance* (4th ed.). Cambridge, MA: Harvard Business Press.

Engelmann, S. E., & Engelmann, K. E. (2004). Impediments to scaling up effective comprehensive school reform models. In T. K. Glennan Jr., S. J. Bodilly, J. R. Galegher, & K. A. Kerr (Eds.), *Expanding the reach of education reforms* (pp. 107–133). Santa Monica, CA: RAND.

Epstein, J. L., & Sheldon, S. B. (2002). Present and accounted for: Improving student attendance through family and community involvement. *Journal of Educational Research, 95,* 308–318.

Evans, R. (2001). *The human side of school change: Reform, resistance, and real-life problems of innovation.* San Francisco: Jossey-Bass.

Fernandez, K. E. (2006). *Clark County School District study of the effectiveness of school improvement plans (SESIP).* Las Vegas, NV: Clark County School District.

Ferrero, D. J. (2006, May). Having it all. *Education Leadership, 63*(8), 8–14.

Finn, P. (1999). *Literacy with an attitude: Educating working-class children in their own self-interest.* Albany: State University of New York Press.

Firestone, W. A., & Corbett, H. D. (1988). Planned organizational change. In N. J. Boyan (Ed.), *Handbook of research on educational administration* (pp. 321–340). New York: Longman.

Fuchs, D., & Fuchs, L. S. (2001, September/October). Responsiveness-to-intervention: A blueprint for practitioners, policymakers, and parents. *Exceptional Children, 38*(1), 57–61.

Fuhrman, S. H. (Ed.). (1993). *Designing coherent education policy: Improving the system.* San Francisco: Jossey-Bass.

Fullan, M. (1999). *Change forces: The sequel.* Philadelphia: Falmer Press.

Fullan, M. (2001a). *The new meaning of educational change* (3rd ed.). New York: Teachers College Press.

Fullan, M. (2001b). *Leading in a culture of change.* San Francisco: Jossey-Bass.

Fullan, M. (2003). *Change forces with a vengeance.* New York: RoutledgeFalmer.

Fullan, M. (2005). *Leadership & sustainability: System thinkers in action.* Thousand Oaks, CA: Corwin Press.

Fullan, M., & Hargreaves, A. (1996). *What's worth fighting for in your school?* New York: Teachers College Press.

Fullan, M., Hill, P., & Crévola, C. (2006). *Breakthrough.* Thousand Oaks, CA: Corwin Press.

Garcia, M. E. (2006). *The effects of whole school reform on instructional program coherence in urban elementary schools.* Unpublished doctoral dissertation, Seton Hall University.

Garden City Elementary. (2009). *Garden City implementation grid—sample items.* Indianapolis, IN: Metropolitan School District of Wayne Township.

Garmston, R. J., & Wellman, B. M. (1999). *The adaptive school: A sourcebook for developing collaborative groups.* Norwood, MA: Christopher-Gordon.

Gladwell, M. (2008). *Outliers: The story of success.* New York: Little, Brown and Company.

Goddard, R. D., Hoy, W. K., & Hoy, A. W. (2000, Summer). Collective teacher efficacy: Its meaning, measure, and impact on student achievement. *American Educational Research Journal, 37,* 479–507.

Goddard, Y. L., Goddard, R. D., & Tschannen-Moran, M. (2007). A theoretical and empirical investigation of teacher collaboration for school improvement and student achievement in public elementary schools. *Teachers College Record, 109,* 877–896.

Goleman, D. (1997). *Emotional intelligence: Why it can matter more than IQ.* New York: Bantam Books.

Goleman, D., Boyatzis, R., & McKee, A. (2001). *Primal leadership: Realizing the power of emotional intelligence.* Boston: Harvard Business School Press.

Gonzales, P., Guzmán, J. C., Partelow, L., Pahlke, E., Jocelyn, L., Kastberg, D., et al. (2004). *Highlights from the Trends in International Mathematics and Science Study 2003.* Washington, DC: U.S. Department of Education, Institute of Education Sciences.

Goodwin, D. (2006, October 29). *Used phones drive third world wireless boom: Rising numbers are landing in places like Bolivia, Jamaica and Kenya.* Accessed at www.msnbc.msn.com/id/15434609 on February, 24, 2009.

Gove, P. B. (Ed.). (1986). *Webster's third new international dictionary of English language unabridged.* Springfield, MA: Merriam-Webster.

Gresham, F. (2001, August). *Response to intervention: An alternative approach to the identification of learning disabilities.* Paper presented at the Learning Disabilities Summit: Building a Foundation for the Future, Washington, DC.

Grigg, W., Lauko, M., & Brockway, D. (2006). *The nation's report card: Science 2005* (NCES 2006-466). Washington, DC: Government Printing Office.

Giuliani, R. (2002). *Leadership.* New York: Miramax Books.

Guskey, T. R. (2002, March). Does it make a difference? Evaluating professional development. *Educational Leadership, 59*(6), pp. 45–51.

Guskey, T. R. (2007). Using assessments to improve teaching and learning. In D. Reeves (Ed.), *Ahead of the curve: The power of assessments to transform teaching and learning* (pp. 15–29). Bloomington, IN: Solution Tree Press.

Hackman, J. R. (2002). *Leading teams: Setting the stage for great performances.* Boston: Harvard Business School Press.

Halachmi, A. (1986). Strategic planning and management: Not necessarily. *Public Productivity Review, 40,* 35–50.

Hall, G., & Galluzzo, G. (1991). *Changing policy into practice: School-based decisionmaking.* Charleston, WV: Appalachia Educational Laboratory. (ERIC Document Reproduction Service No. ED346563)

Hall, G. E., & Hord, S. M. (1987). *Change in schools: Facilitating the process.* Albany: State University of New York Press.

Hall, G. E., & Hord, S. M. (2006). *Implementing change: Patterns, principles, and potholes* (2nd ed.). Boston: Pearson.

Hallmarks of Excellence. (2007). *Personal results workbook.* Indianapolis, IN: Chorus.

Hanson, R. A., & Schutz, R. E. (1986, Spring). A comparison of methods for measuring achievement in basic skills program evaluation. *Educational Evaluation and Policy Analysis, 8,* 101–113.

Hanushek, E. A., & Raymond, M. E. (2005). Does school accountability lead to improved student performance? *Journal of Policy Analysis and Management, 24,* 297–327.

Hastings and Prince Edward District School Board. (2007). *Hastings and Prince Edward District School Board School Improvement Plan Template.* Belleville, Ontario, Canada: Author.

Hattie, J. (1992, April). Measuring the effects of schooling. *Australian Journal of Education, 36*(1), 5–13.

Havelock, R. G. (1971). *Planning for innovation through dissemination and utilization of knowledge.* Ann Arbor: University of Michigan, Center for Research on Utilization of Scientific Knowledge.

Haycock, K. (2008, October 24). *Raising achievement and closing gaps between groups: Lessons from schools on the performance frontier.* Presentation to Illinois Superintendents, Springfield, IL. Accessed at www2.edtrust.org/NR/rdonlyres/%205613FC9B-CF6B-43A8-993B-2E6EC052D0F8/0/ilsupes2008.pdf on November 10, 2008.

Heacox, D. (2002). *Differentiating instruction in the regular classroom: How to reach and teach all learners, grades 3–12*. Minneapolis, MN: Free Spirit.

Heifetz, R. A., & Linsky, M. (2002). *Leadership on the line*. Boston: Harvard Business School Press.

Hill, J. D., & Flynn, K. M. (2006). *Classroom instruction that works with English language learners*. Alexandria, VA: Association for Supervision and Curriculum Development.

Holliday, W. G. (2001, February). Getting teachers to change. *Science Scope, 24*(5), 56–59.

Hopkins, D. (2001). *School improvement for real*. New York: RoutledgeFalmer.

Hopkins, D., & West, M. (2002). Evaluation as school improvement: A developmental perspective from England. In D. Nevo (Ed.), *School-based evaluation: An international perspective: Vol. 8* (pp. 89–112). London: Emerald Group.

Hord, S. M. (1997). *Professional learning communities: Communities of continuous inquiry and improvement*. Austin, TX: Southwest Educational Development Laboratory.

Horine, J. E., Frazier, M. A., & Edmister, R. O. (1998). The Baldrige as a framework for assessing leadership practices. *Planning and Changing, 29*(1), 2–23.

House, E. R. (1981). Three perspectives on innovation. In R. Lehming & M. Kane (Eds.), *Improving schools: Using what we know* (pp. 17–41). Thousand Oaks, CA: SAGE.

Howley, C. (2001, April). *To continue, press on: Sustaining school improvement*. Paper presented at the Annual Meeting of the American Educational Research Association, Seattle, WA.

Hoye, J. D., & Stern, D. (2008, September 10). The career academy story: A case study of how research can move policy and practice. *Education Week, 28*(3), 24–26.

Hunter, M. (1982). *Mastery teaching: Increasing instructional effectiveness in elementary, secondary schools, colleges and universities*. Thousand Oaks, CA: Corwin Press.

Index of the Web. (n.d.). *Automobile Manufacturers*. Accessed at www.indexoftheweb.com/Automobile/Manufacturers.htm on February 1, 2009.

Jenlink, P. M. (Ed.). (1995). *Systemic change: Touchstones for the future school*. Arlington Heights, IL: Iri/Skylight.

Jenlink, P. M., Reigeluth, C. M., Carr, A. A., & Nelson, L. M. (1996, January/February). An expedition for change: Facilitating the systemic change process in school districts. *TechTrends, 41*(1), 21–30.

Johnson, P. E., & Scollay, S. J. (2001). School-based, decision-making councils—Conflict, leader power and social influence in the vertical team. *Journal of Educational Administration, 39*, 47–66.

Jones, M., & Yonezawa, S. (2008, December/2009, January). Student-driven research. *Educational Leadership, 66*(4), 65–69.

Kannapel, P. J., & Clements, S. K. (with Taylor, D., & Hibpshman, T.). (2005, February). *Inside the black box of high-performing high-poverty schools: A report from the Prichard Committee for Academic Excellence*. Lexington, KY: Prichard Committee for Academic Excellence. Accessed at www.cdl.org/resource-library/pdf/FordReportJE.pdf on October 16, 2008.

Kaplan, R. S., & Norton, D. P. (2005). The office of strategy management. *Harvard Business Review, 83*(10), 72–80.

Katzenbach, J. R., & Smith, D. K. (1993). *The wisdom of teams: Creating the high-performance organization.* New York: Harper Business School Press.

Kelly, K. (2009). The expansion of ignorance. *The Technium.* Accessed at www.kk.org/thetechnium/archives /2008/10/the_expansion_o.php on February 23, 2009.

Kentucky Department of Education. (2008). *School & district improvement planning checking implementation & impact.* Frankfort, KY: Author. Accessed at www.education.ky.gov/KDE/Administrative+ Resources/School+Improvement/Comprehensive+Improvement+Planning/Implementation+and+Im pact+Checks.htm on March 1, 2008.

Kidron, Y., & Darwin, M. (2007, Spring). A systemic review of whole school improvement models. *Journal of Education for Students Placed at Risk, 12*(1), 9–35.

Koch, R. (1998). *The 80/20 principle: The secret of achieving more with less.* New York: Doubleday Press.

Koch, C. (2009). *School improvement plan and resources: 2009–10.* Springfield: Illinois State Board of Education. Accessed at www.isbe.net/sos/htmls/school.htm on February 6, 2009.

Kotler, P., & Murphy, P. E. (1981). Strategic planning for higher education. *Journal of Higher Education, 52,* 470–489.

Kouzes, J. M., & Posner, B. Z. (1995). *The leadership challenge: How to keep getting extraordinary things done in organizations* (2nd ed.). San Francisco: Jossey-Bass.

Langer, G. M., Colton, A. B., & Goff, L. S. (2003). *Collaborative analysis of student work: Improving teaching and learning.* Alexandria, VA: Association for Supervision and Curriculum Development.

Leadership and Learning Center. (2005a). *Sample Hillsboro, Oregon, school improvement template and plan.* Englewood, CO: Author.

Leadership and Learning Center. (2005b). *Planning, implementation, and monitoring framework.* Englewood, CO: Author.

Leadership and Learning Center. (2007a, December). *Executive summary of Ontario's school board improvement plans: The PIM analysis.* Englewood, CO: Author.

Leadership and Learning Center. (2007b, December). *Planning, implementation, and monitoring (PIM) summary—Houston Independent School District.* Paper presented to Houston school administrators, Englewood, CO.

Leadership and Learning Center. (2008, April). *An analysis of select school improvement plans within the province of Ontario, Canada.* Paper presented to the Literacy and Numeracy Secretariat, Toronto, Ontario, Canada.

Leadership Strategies. (n.d.). *Strategic plan assessment.* Accessed at www.leadstrat.com/facil-strategic -plan-assessment.html on August 21, 2008.

Leithwood, K. A., & Riehl, C. (2003, November). *What do we already know about successful school leadership.* Paper presented to the AERA Division A Task Force on Developing Research in Educational Leadership, Chicago.

Leithwood, K., Jantzi, D., & Steinbach, R. (1999). *Changing leadership for changing times.* Philadelphia: Open University Press.

Lencioni, P. (1998). *The five temptations of a CEO: A leadership fable.* San Francisco: Jossey-Bass.

Lencioni, P. (2004). *Death by meeting: A leadership fable about solving the most painful problem in business.* San Francisco: Jossey-Bass.

Lencioni, P. (2005). *Overcoming the five dysfunctions of a team: A field guide for leaders, managers, and facilitators.* San Francisco: Jossey-Bass.

Lencioni, P. (2006). *Silos, politics, & turf wars: A leadership fable about destroying the barriers that turn colleagues into competitors.* San Francisco: Jossey-Bass.

Lencioni, P. (2007). *The three signs of a miserable job: A fable for managers (and their employees).* San Francisco: Jossey-Bass.

Levine, D. U., & Lezotte, L. W. (1990). *Unusually effective schools: A review and analysis of research and practice.* Madison, WI: National Center for Effective Schools Research and Development.

Levine, D. U., & Leibert, R. E. (1987, March). Improving school improvement plans. *Elementary School Journal, 87,* 397–412.

Lewis, A. (2009). *School improvement rubric review.* Las Vegas: Clark County School District Research and School Improvement Department.

Lewis, C. (2006). *School improvement in action: Lessons in sustainability.* Kelowna, British Columbia, Canada: Society for the Advancement of Excellence in Education.

Lezotte, L. W. (1984, April). *School effective research: A tribute to Ron Edmonds. "One Perspective on an Effective Schools Research Agenda."* Paper presented at the Annual Meeting of the American Educational Research Association, New Orleans, LA. (ERIC Document Reproduction Service No. ED252961)

Lezotte, L. W. (1997). *Learning for all.* Okemos, MI: Effective Schools Products.

Lezotte, L. W. (2008). *Correlates of effective schools: The first and second generation.* Okemos, MI: Effective Schools Products.

Lezotte, L. W., & Bancroft, B. A. (1985, Summer). School improvement based on effective schools research: A promising approach for economically disadvantaged and minority students. *Journal of Negro Education, 54,* 301–312.

Lezotte, L. W., & McKee, K. (2006). *Stepping up: Leading the charge to improve our schools.* Okemos, MI: Effective Schools Products.

Libby, M. T., Piper, M. F., & Sandbothe, S. P. (2005). Professional development and accountability: Linking best practices in education and the private sector to create an evaluation framework (Doctoral dissertation, Saint Louis University, 2005). *Dissertations Abstracts International, 67*(03), 799A.

Liontos, L. B. (1994). *Shared decision-making.* Eugene, OR: ERIC Clearinghouse on Educational Management. (ERIC Document Reproduction Service No. ED368034)

Lipton, L., & Wellman, B. (with Humbard, C.). (2001). *Mentoring matters: A practical guide to learning-focused relationships.* Sherman, CT: MiraVia.

Little, J. W. (1990). The persistence of privacy: Autonomy and initiative in teachers' professional relations. *Teachers College Record, 91,* 509–536.

Lunenburg, F. C., & Ornstein, A. C. (2000). *Educational administration: Concepts and practices* (3rd ed.). Belmont, CA: Wadsworth/Thompson Learning.

Lynch, R., & Marrs, R. (2009). *Strategic alliances: THE NEXT GENERATION.* Providence, RI: Warren Company. Accessed at www.warrenco.com/Strategic_Alliances-TNG_V3_Announcement_without_appendices _Final_7-10-07.pdf on February 14, 2009.

Mann, D. (1975, March). *The field study of programs for educational change.* Washington, DC: American Educational Research Association.

Manzo, K. K. (2008, August 27). Writing to learn. *Education Week, 28*(3), 23–25.

Martin, M. O., Mullis, I., Gregory, K. D., Hoyle, C., & Shen, C. (2000). *Effective schools in science and mathematics.* Chestnut Hill, MA: TIMMS International Study Center.

Marsden, M. J. (1991). Evaluation: Towards a definition and statement of purpose. *Australian Journal of Educational Technology, 7,* 31–38.

Marx, G. (2006). *Future-focused leadership: Preparing schools, students, and communities for tomorrow's realities.* Alexandria, VA: Association for Supervision and Curriculum Development.

Marzano, R. J. (2000). *Transforming classroom grading.* Alexandria, VA: Association for Supervision and Curriculum Development.

Marzano, R. J. (2001). *Designing a new taxonomy of educational objectives.* Thousand Oaks, CA: Corwin Press.

Marzano, R. J. (2003). *What works in schools: Translating research into action.* Alexandria, VA: Association for Supervision and Curriculum Development.

Marzano, R. J. (2007). *The art and science of teaching: A comprehensive framework for effective instruction.* Alexandria, VA: Association for Supervision and Curriculum Development.

Marzano, R. J., & Kendall, J. S., (with Gaddy, B. B.). (1999). *Essential knowledge: The debate over what American students should know.* Aurora, CO: Mid-continent Research for Education and Learning.

Marzano, R. J., Norford, J. S., Paynter, D. E., Pickering, D. J., & Gaddy, B. B. (2001). *A handbook for classroom instruction that works.* Alexandria, VA: Association for Supervision and Curriculum Development.

Marzano, R. J., Pickering, D. J., & Pollock, J. E. (2001). *Classroom instruction that works: Research-based strategies for increasing student achievement.* Alexandria, VA: Association for Supervision and Curriculum Development.

Marzano, R. J., Waters, T., & McNulty, B. A. (2005). *School leadership that works: From research to results.* Alexandria, VA: Association for Supervision and Curriculum Development.

Mattingley, R. (2008, September). *Effective planning for continuous school improvement.* PowerPoint presentation to Ontario School Boards Literacy and Numeracy Secretariat, Toronto, Ontario, Canada.

McClure, R., & Johnson, J. F., Jr. (1997). *Successful Texas schoolwide programs: Suggestions for technical assistance providers.* Austin: Charles A. Dana Center at the University of Texas.

McDonald, J. P., Mohr, N., Dichter, A., & McDonald, E. C. (2007). *The power of protocols: An educator's guide to better practice* (2nd ed.). New York: Teachers College Press.

McLaughlin, M. (1990, December). The RAND change agent study revisited: Macro perspectives and micro realities. *Educational Researcher, 19*(9), 11–16.

McNamara, C. (2007). *Field guide to nonprofit strategic planning and facilitation* (3rd ed.). Minneapolis, MN: Authenticity Consulting.

McNelis, R. H. (1998). *The school improvement plan as a model school-level for accountability: An investigation of Pittsburgh Public Schools planning requirements.* Unpublished doctoral dissertation, University of Pittsburgh.

Miller, C. C., & Cardinal, L. B. (1994, December). Strategic planning and firm performance: A synthesis of more than two decades of research. *Academy of Management Journal, 37,* 1649–1665.

Mintrop, H., MacLellan, A. M., & Quintero, M. F. (2001, April). School improvement plans in schools on probation: A comparative content analysis across three accountability systems. *Educational Administration Quarterly, 37,* 197–218.

Mintzberg, H. (1994). *The rise and fall of strategic planning: Reconceiving roles for planning, plans, planners.* New York: Free Press.

Mitchell, S. M. (1995). Enabling good teaching performance: Performance management in education. In S. B. Bacharach & B. Mundell (Eds.), *Images of schools structures and roles in organizational behavior* (pp. 201–238). Thousand Oaks, CA: Corwin Press.

Montgomery, D. (2009). *Hillsboro, Oregon, school improvement template.* Hillsboro, OR: Hillsboro School District 1J.

Morrison, K. (1998). *Management theories for educational change.* Thousand Oaks, CA: SAGE.

Mukilteo School Board. (2006, November 13). School improvement plans, 2005–07. *Cover sheet for business of the board.* Mukilteo, WA: Mukilteo School District No. 6. Accessed at www.mukilteo.wednet.edu/board/BrdPacket/2006_07/06_11_13Packet/SIP_BriefingPaper.html on February 12, 2009.

Murphy, C. U., & Lick, D. W. (2001). *Whole-faculty study groups: Creating student-based professional development* (2nd ed.). Thousand Oaks, CA: Corwin Press.

Murphy, J. (1990). The educational reform movement of the 1980s: A comprehensive analysis. In J. Murphy (Ed.), *The educational reform movement of the 1980s: Perspectives and cases* (pp. 3–55). Berkley, CA: McCutchan.

National Center for Education Statistics. (2000, December). *Monitoring school quality: An indicators report.* Washington, DC: U.S. Department of Education.

National Council of Teachers of Mathematics. (2006). *Professional and standards for teaching mathematics.* Reston, VA: Author. Accessed at http://standards.nctm.org on February 23, 2006.

National Research Council. (1998). *National science education standards.* Washington, DC: National Academy Press.

National School Boards Association. (2002, August). *No Child Left Behind Act: Policy guidelines for local school boards.* Washington, DC: National School Boards Association.

National Staff Development Council. (2001). *NSDC's standards for staff development.* Oxford, OH: Confederation of Oregon School Administrators.

National Study of School Evaluation. (2003). *System-wide improvement: Focusing on student learning.* Schaumburg, IL: Author.

Natrona County School District No. 1. (2000). *Shared decision-making.* Casper, WY: Author.

Neale, D. C., Bailey, W. J., & Ross, B. E. (1981). *Strategies for school improvement: Cooperative planning and organization development.* Needham Heights, MA: Allyn & Bacon.

Ohio Leadership Advisory Council. (2008, January). *Leadership development framework.* Columbus, OH: Author.

Pak Tee, N. (2003, January). The Singapore school and the school excellence model. *Educational Research for Policy and Practice, 2,* 27–39.

Peters, T. (1987). *Thriving on chaos: Handbook for a management revolution.* New York: Knopf.

Pfeffer, J., & Sutton, R. I. (2000). *The knowing-doing gap: How smart companies turn knowledge into action.* Boston: Harvard Business School Press.

Pfeffer, J., & Sutton, R. I. (2006). *Hard facts, dangerous half-truths, and total nonsense: Profiting from evidence-based management.* Boston: Harvard Business School Press.

Phillips, P. A., & Moutinho, L. (2000, May). The strategic planning index: A tool for measuring strategic planning effectiveness. *Journal of Travel Research, 38,* 369–379.

Popham, W. J. (2003). *Test better, teach better: The instructional role of assessment.* Alexandria, VA: Association for Supervision and Curriculum Development.

Popham, W. J. (2008). *Transformative assessment.* Alexandria, VA: Association for Supervision and Curriculum Development.

Poynter Middle School. (2006). *2006–07 school improvement plan.* Hillsboro, OR: Author.

Putnam, R. (1993, August). Unlocking organizational routines that prevent learning. *The systems thinker: Building shared understanding, 4*(6), 1–4.

Quinn, R. E. (2004). *Building the bridge as you walk on it: A guide for leading change.* San Francisco: Jossey-Bass.

Reames, E., & Spencer, W. (1998, April). *Teacher efficacy and commitment: Relationships to middle school culture.* Paper presented at the annual meeting of the American Educational Research Association, San Diego, CA.

Reeves, D. B. (2002a). *The daily disciplines of leadership: How to improve student achievement, staff motivation, and personal organization.* San Francisco: Jossey-Bass.

Reeves, D. B. (2002b). *Making standards work: How to implement standards-based assessments in the classroom, school, and district* (3rd ed.). Denver, CO: Advanced Learning Press.

Reeves, D. B. (2002c). *The leader's guide to standards: A blueprint for educational equity and excellence.* San Francisco: Jossey-Bass.

Reeves, D. B. (2002d). *Holistic accountability: Serving students, schools, and community.* Thousand Oaks, CA: Corwin Press.

Reeves, D. B. (2003). *High performance in high poverty schools: 90/90/90 and beyond.* Englewood, CO: Center for Performance Assessment. Accessed at www.sabine.k12.la.us/online/leadershipacademy/high%20 performance%2090%2090%2090%20and%20beyond.pdf on October 14, 2008.

Reeves, D. B. (2004a). *Assessing educational leaders: Evaluating performance for improved individual and organizational results.* Thousand Oaks, CA: Corwin Press.

Reeves, D. B. (2004b). *Accountability in action: A blueprint for learning organizations* (2nd ed). Englewood, CO: Advanced Learning Press.

Reeves, D. B. (2006). *The learning leader: How to focus school improvement for better results.* Alexandria, VA: Association for Supervision and Curriculum Development.

Reeves, D. B. (Ed.). (2007). *Ahead of the curve: The power of assessment to transform teaching and learning.* Bloomington, IN: Solution Tree Press.

Reeves, D. B. (2008a). *Reframing teacher leadership to improve your school.* Alexandria, VA: Association for Supervision and Curriculum Development.

Reeves, D. B. (2008b, February). Leading to change: Effective grading practices. *Educational Leadership, 65*(5), 85–87.

Reeves, D. B. (2009a). *Assessing educational leaders: Evaluating performance for improved individual and organizational results* (2nd ed.). Thousand Oaks, CA: Corwin Press.

Reeves, D. B. (2009b). *Leading change in your school.* Alexandria, VA: Association for Supervision and Curriculum Development.

Reeves, D., Smith, R., White, S., Peery, A., Mueller, J., & Caldwell, N. (2007). *Achievement, equity, and leadership 2007: Clark County School District commitment to success.* Englewood, CO: Center for Performance Assessment.

Reynolds, D. & Teddlie, C. (with Hopkins, D., & Stringfield, S.). (2000). Linking school improvement and school effectiveness. In C. Teddlie & D. Reynolds (Eds.), *The international handbook of school effectiveness research* (pp. 206–210). London: Falmer Press.

Rogers, E. (1995). *Diffusion of Innovations.* New York: Free Press.

Ronka, D., Lachat, M. A., Slaughter, R., & Meltzer, J. (2008, December/2009, January). Answering the questions that count. *Educational Leadership, 66*(4), 18–22.

Rosenholtz, S. (1989). *Teachers' workplace: The social organization of schools.* New York: Longman.

Rosenshine, B. (1976, March). Recent research on teaching behaviors and student achievement. *Journal of Teacher Education, 27,* 61–64.

Russell, M., Takac, P., & Usher, L. (2004). Industry productivity trends under the North American Industry Classification system. *Monthly Labor Review, 127*(11), 31–42.

Rushkoff, D. (2005). *Get back in the box: Innovation from the inside out.* New York: HarperCollins.

Sagor, R. (2000). *Guiding school improvement with action research.* Alexandria, VA: Association for Supervision and Curriculum Development.

Sammons, P., Hillman, J., & Mortimore, P. (1995). *Key characteristics of effective schools: A review of school effectiveness research.* London: Institute of Education.

Saphier, J., Bigda-Peyton, T., & Pierson, G. (1989). *How to make decisions that stay made.* Alexandria, VA: Association for Supervision and Curriculum Development.

Sarason, S. B. (1996). *Revisiting "the culture of the school and the problem of change."* New York: Teachers College Press.

Sashkin, M., & Egermeier, J. (1993). *School change models and processes: A review and synthesis of research and practice.* Washington, DC: U.S. Department of Education, Office of Educational Research and Improvement, Programs for the Improvement of Practice.

Scheeler, M. C., Ruhl, K. L., & McAfee, J. K. (2004). Providing performance feedback to teachers: A review. *Teacher Education and Special Education, 27,* 396–407.

Schlecty, P. C. (2000). *Shaking up the school house: How to support and sustain educational innovation.* San Francisco: Jossey-Bass.

Schmoker, M. (1999). *Results: The key to continuous improvement* (2nd ed.). Alexandria, VA: Association for Supervision and Curriculum Development.

Schmoker, M. (2001). *The results fieldbook: Practical strategies from dramatically improved schools.* Alexandria, VA: Association for Supervision and Curriculum Development.

Schmoker, M. (2004, February). Tipping point: From feckless reform to substantive instructional improvement. *Phi Delta Kappan, 85,* 424–432.

Schmoker, M. (2006). *Results now: How we can achieve unprecedented improvements in teaching and learning.* Alexandria, VA: Association for Supervision and Curriculum Development.

Scholtes, P. R. (with Joiner, B. L., & Streibel, B. J.). (2001). *The team handbook: How to use teams to improve quality* (2nd ed.). Madison, WI: Oriel.

Schön, D. A. (1987). *Educating the reflective practitioner: Toward a new design for teaching and learning in the professions.* San Francisco: Jossey-Bass.

School Library Journal. (2008). Has NCLB helped student achievement? *School Library Journal.* Accessed at www.schoollibraryjournal.com/article/CA6573876.html on July 24, 2008.

Schwartz, P. (1991). *The art of the long view: Planning for the future in an uncertain world.* New York: Doubleday.

Seivers, L. C. (2007, August). *Tennessee School Improvement Planning Process.* Nashville: Tennessee Department of Education.

Senge, P. M. (1990). *The fifth discipline: The art and practice of the learning organization.* New York: Doubleday.

Senge, P. M. (2000). *Schools that learn: A fifth discipline fieldbook for educators, parents, and everyone who cares about education.* New York: Doubleday.

Shaughnessy, M. F. (2004, June). An interview with Anita Woolfolk: The educational psychology of teacher efficacy. *Educational Psychology Review, 16,* 153–176.

Sizer, T. R. (2004). *The red pencil: Convictions from experience in education.* New Haven, CT: Yale University Press.

Smith, J., & O'Day, J. (1991). Systemic school reform. In S. H. Fuhrman & B. Malen (Eds.), *The politics of curriculum and testing: The 1990 yearbook of the Politics of Education Association* (pp. 233–267). London: Falmer.

Sosik, J. J., & Dionne, S. D. (1997, June). Leadership styles and Deming's behavior factors. *Journal of Business and Psychology, 11,* 447–462.

Sparks, D. (1998, April). *Teacher expertise linked to student learning: Virtually all their teachers must be learning virtually all the time.* Accessed at www.nsdc.org/news/results/4-98sparks.cfm on September 3, 2008.

Sparks, D. (2004a, March). *Closing the knowing-doing gap requires acting on what we already know.* Oxford, OH: National Staff Development Council. Accessed at www.nsdc.org/news/results/res3-04spar.cfm on February 17, 2007.

Sparks, D. (2004b, Winter). A call to creativity: It's time for us to take the lead in creating change. *Journal of Staff Development, 25*(1), 54–62.

Springboard Schools. (2006). *Minding the gap: New role for school districts in the age of accountability.* San Francisco: Author.

Steiner, L. (2000). *A review of the research literature on scaling up in education: The problem of scaling-up in education.* Chicago: North Central Regional Educational Laboratory.

Sternberg, R. J., & Horvath, J. A. (1995, August). A prototype view of expert teaching. *Educational Researcher, 24*(6), 9–17.

Stout Field Elementary. (2009). *Strategic and continuous school improvement plan.* Indianapolis, IN: Metropolitan School District of Wayne Township.

Strong, R. W., Silver, H. F., & Perini, M. J. (2001). *Teaching what matters most: Standards and strategies for raising student achievement.* Alexandria, VA: Association for Supervision and Curriculum Development.

Sugai, G., & Horner, R. (2002). The evolution of discipline practices: School-wide positive behavior supports. *Child & Family Behavior Therapy, 24*(1/2), 23–50.

Surowiecki, J. (2004). *The wisdom of crowds: Why the many are smarter than the few and how collective wisdom shapes business, economies, societies, and nations.* New York: Doubleday.

Thomas B. Fordham Institute & the Broad Foundation. (2003). *Better leaders for America's schools: A manifesto.* Accessed at www.edexcellence.net/doc/manifesto.pdf on February 13, 2009.

Tilman, L. C. (Ed.). (2009). *The SAGE handbook of African American education.* Thousand Oaks, CA: SAGE.

Tomlinson, C. A., Kaplan, S. N., Renzulli, J. S., Purcell, J. H., Leppien, J. H., & Burns, D. E., et al. (2002). *The parallel curriculum: A design to develop high potential and challenge high-ability learners.* Thousand Oaks, CA: Corwin Press.

Training and Development Agency for Schools. (2008). *The school improvement planning process framework.* Accessed at www.tda.gov.uk/remodelling/extendedschools/sipf2/process.aspx on December 14, 2008.

Tucker, M. S., & Codding, J. B. (1998). *Standards for our schools: How to set them, measure them, and reach them.* San Francisco: Jossey-Bass.

Viadero, D. (2006, August). Cognition studies offer insights on academic tactics. *Education Week, 26*(1), 12–13.

Wagner, T., & Kegan, R., (2005). *Change leadership: A practical guide to transforming our schools.* San Francisco: Jossey-Bass.

Wedl, R. J., & Schroeder, J. (2005, July). *Response to intervention: An alternative to traditional eligibility criteria for students with disabilities.* St. Paul, MN: Center for Policy Studies, Hamline University.

Weick, K. E. (1976, March). Educational organizations as loosely-coupled systems. *Administrative Science Quarterly, 21*, 1–19.

Weiss, H. (1991). *Maps: Getting from here to there.* New York: Houghton Mifflin.

Weiss, J. (2008). *Does a shared decision making model improve student achievement? Implications for leadership.* Unpublished doctoral dissertation, Loyola University, Chicago.

Wenglinsky, H. (2002, February 13). How schools matter: The link between teacher classroom practices and student academic performance. *Education Policy Analysis Archives, 10*(12), 6–31.

Wheatley, M. J. (2005). *Finding our way: Leadership for an uncertain time.* San Francisco: Barrett-Kohler.

White, S. H. (2005a). *Beyond the numbers: Making data work for teachers & school leaders.* Englewood, CO: Advanced Learning Press.

White, S. H. (2005b). *Show me the proof! Tools and strategies to make data work for you.* Englewood, CO: Advanced Learning Press.

White, S. H. (2005c, Fall). Try another way: Ten practical strategies to make high schools work. *Insight: Texas Association of School Administrators Professional Journal, 20*(2), 25–28.

White, S. H. (2006, Spring). Don't wait to replicate. *Maryland Association for Supervision and Curriculum Development Journal,* 19–25.

White, S., & Smith, R. (2006). [Review of school improvement plans]. Unpublished raw data.

Wiggins, G., & McTighe, J. (2005). *Understanding by design* (2nd ed.). Alexandria, VA: Association for Supervision and Curriculum Development.

Wolcott, H. F. (1990). *Writing up qualitative research: Vol. 20. Qualitative Research Methods Series.* Newbury Park, CA: Sage.

Yeh, S. S. (2007, December). The cost-effectiveness of five policies for improving student achievement. *American Journal of Evaluation, 28,* 416–436.

Ylimaki, R. M., Jacobson, S. L., & Drysdale, L. (2007). Making a difference in challenging, high-poverty schools: Successful principals in the USA, England, and Australia. *School Effectiveness and School Improvement, 18,* 361–381.

York, J. (1992, October). Productivity in wood containers. *Monthly Labor Review, 115*(10), 16–19. Accessed at http://www.bls.gov/opub/mlr/1992/10/art3full.pdf on June 4, 2008.

Zemelman, S., Daniels, H., & Hyde, A. (2005). *Best practice: Today's standards for teaching and learning in America's school* (3rd ed.). Portsmouth, NH: Heinemann.

Zook, C., & Allen, J. (2001). *Profit from the core: Growth strategy in an era of turbulence.* Boston: Harvard Business School Press.

Zook, S., Oker, K., & Cerauli, L. (2008). *Hawthorn School Improvement Template.* Vernon Hills, IL: Hawthorn School District 73.

Index

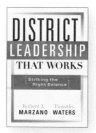

District Leadership That Works: Striking the Right Balance
Robert J. Marzano and Timothy Waters
Bridge the divide between administrative duties and daily classroom impact with a leadership mechanism called "defined autonomy." Learn strategies for creating district-defined goals while giving building-level staff the stylistic freedom to respond quickly and effectively to student failure. **BKF314**

The High-Performing School: Benchmarking the 10 Indicators of Effectiveness
Mardale Dunsworth and Dawn Billings
Become a high-performing school by implementing the on-site school review—a cooperative venture between an external review team and a school's administrators, teachers, and students. **BKF294**

Ahead of the Curve: The Power of Assessment to Transform Teaching and Learning
Edited by Douglas Reeves
Get the anthology that offers the ideas and recommendations of many of the world's leaders in assessment. Many perspectives of effective assessment design and implementation culminate in a call for redirecting assessment to improve student achievement and inform instruction. **BKF232**

On Excellence in Teaching
Edited by Robert J. Marzano
Learn from the world's best education researchers, theorists, and staff developers. The authors' diverse expertise delivers a wide range of theories and strategies and provides a comprehensive view of effective instruction from a theoretical, systemic, and classroom perspective. **BKF278**

On Common Ground: The Power of Professional Learning Communities
Edited by Richard DuFour, Robert Eaker, and Rebecca DuFour
Examine a colorful cross-section of educators' experiences with PLCs. This collection of insights and stories from practitioners throughout North America highlights the benefits of a PLC and offers unique angles of approach to a variety of school improvement challenges. **BKF180**

Change Wars
Edited by Michael Fullan and Andy Hargreaves
What can organizations do to create profound, enduring changes? The third anthology in the Leading Edge™ series explores why traditional change strategies have failed and examines constructive alternatives. International experts share their theories-in-action on how to achieve deep change. **BKF254**

Solution Tree | Press *a division of* Solution Tree   Visit solution-tree.com or call 800.733.6786 to order.